The Tai Chi Companion

a book around tai chi

by Lucy Gardner

A collection of information and exercises
to accompany you on your tai chi path

photography by Frederick Behar

First published in 2015 by Warbler Publications

warble98@gmail.com

Printed in Great Britain

ISBN-13: 978-1517481278

Disclaimer

Please note that the author and publisher of this book are not responsible in any manner whatsoever for any injury that may result from practising the techniques and/or following the instructions given. Since the physical activities described herein may be too strenuous in nature for some readers to engage in safely, it is essential that you consult a doctor prior to training.

Acknowledgements

The exercises in this book came from a variety of sources. Some were the result of research, others I absorbed over years practising with teachers and students of tai chi around the world. Still more were my own creation.

Two men in particular have been of great help to me. My first teacher, Douglas Hardie from the Scottish Highlands, whose patience and enthusiasm started me on my tai chi path. Also Master Yang Dong Bao of Yangshuo, China, a wonderful teacher who showed me most of the exercises included in the warm up section.

But the inspiration and initial encouragement for the book, as well as a great many of the exercises, came from the brilliant Frederick Behar, who searches tirelessly for the essence of tai chi and shares his knowledge openly and generously with anyone smart enough to listen.

Contents

Preface

When I started doing tai chi I discovered a younger, fitter me lurking inside a body which had begun to stiffen and deteriorate, despite the fact that I wasn't yet forty. It's a key time of life for many people, when they start to question their lifestyle and values.

Mentally, we have begun to feel stale, spiritually, there is a void, and physically, our bodies are losing elasticity and flexibility. Even simple tasks such as walking uphill or putting on a tight top can start to feel like an effort.

Like many Westerners, I was struck by the poise and flexibility of seasoned tai chi practitioners, women twenty years older than me who could not only sink to the floor on one leg but get straight back up again and do so gracefully. Once I caught myself groaning when rising from a chair I knew it was time to take action!

So I found a tai chi school and started with once a week classes. I soon began practising at home most days. I sought out more and more classes. I read widely. Within two years I had abandoned my home and marriage. After three years I packed in my job and travelled to China to study tai chi full time.

I haven't gone back to conventional living. One could say that tai chi has had a profound effect on me.

In the beginning, though, it was the postural changes which made the biggest difference to me. Doing tai chi (albeit not very ably and without great understanding) brought a physical confidence which allowed me to grow and flourish. You might not want or need to make such radical changes to your life, but tai chi can provide the tools to make it richer and more enjoyable.

This is not a book about tai chi, but rather a book *around* tai chi. There are already lots of books about tai chi, some of them written by people with far greater knowledge and ability than me. I have found that tai chi can be enhanced by giving attention to many other activities which complement it or otherwise help you improve, and it is this knowledge in particular that I want to share.

If you search, you can relate tai chi principles to just about everything. Part 2 includes many physical activities which will help your practice, but also contains guidance which has the potential to bring improvements to all areas of life.

In Part 1 you will find background information on internal Oriental arts and a somewhat irreverent history of tai chi. I've also discussed possible benefits of tai chi, why people might want to take it up, and where that might lead them.

Above all, I've tried to make this guide accessible and stimulating. I hope you will find it a useful companion on your tai chi path.

Introduction

I am regularly struck by how much people in the West are doing wrong. We don't stand correctly, we don't walk naturally, we have poor breathing habits, we constrict our bodies and let them stiffen up through lack of use. We use the wrong muscles through ignorance or laziness, so that we have only a fraction of the range of motion our ancestors benefited from.

To take one example, the Global Burden of Disease 2010 Study found that almost 1 in 10 people Worldwide suffered from lower back pain, with prevalence much higher in Western Europe at 15%.[1] Among the many causes cited for this type of malady are repetitive work, lack of exercise, poor posture, obesity and stress.

There are also many more insidious areas of our lives which are affected by the misuse of our bodies. Everything is related, so that improper breathing affects our posture and in turn our sleep, digestion and mental health. Prolonged use of computers causes the layers of fascia surrounding our muscles to become inflexible, which causes round shoulders, neck ache, headaches, poor posture and so on.

In this and many other ways we are making life harder for ourselves and making physical movement which should be natural and enjoyable difficult and uncomfortable.

So is it any wonder that we view tai chi as a mystical art? Grown up people who can move freely and without pain? A rarity indeed. This may be why the Chinese are able to appear superior, telling us that there are certain things people from the West can never hope to understand or accomplish, and it would be dangerous to even try. In reality it may be just because they've been using squat toilets all their lives.

Read on to learn how you can actually achieve this nirvana, with or without accompanying spiritual enlightenment.

Special Terms

Chinese

Terms are generally given in Pinyin, the official phonetic system for transliterating Chinese characters into the Roman alphabet, except where a different form is more widely used. For example, "tai chi" remains more popular in English speaking countries than the Pinyin "taiji", so I've stuck with the former spelling.

Dantian

In fact we have three Dantians:

- ◆ lower (Xia Dantian or Shen Guan) about two fingers' width below and three fingers' width behind your belly button. It is the body's energy centre and focus of breathing as well as being the centre of gravity when you are standing up.

- ◆ middle (Zhong Dantian or Tan Zhong) at the solar plexus in the centre of your chest   The centre of gravity when you're seated, it is said to be our emotional centre.

- ◆ upper (Shang Dantian or Yin Tang) your third eye, above your nose and behind your forehead. It is considered to be the spiritual gate and home to our wisdom mind.

When people talk about the Dantian without specifying which they normally mean the lower Dantian. Variant spellings include Dantien and Tantien.

Daoyin

"Guiding and stretching". Ancient Taoist qi cultivation exercises; the forerunner of qi gong. Many of today's qi gong series are based on daoyin.

Hui Yin

Acupuncture point "Meeting of Yin" in English or Conception Vessel 1. Situated midway between the anus and sexual organs. This location is thought to be very effective for a number of ailments, and a particularly important yin-strengthening point, but in practise it's used fairly infrequently, on account of its intimate location.

Jing

Essence; life force.

Jin

Any of a number of special sensing abilities used in tai chi. A few examples:

Nei jin (internal power)

Fa jin (explosive force)

Hua jin (neutralising skill)

Dong jin (for understanding the opponent's intentions)

Ting jin (the ability to listen to and understand an opponent's internal state)

Tzan lien jin (the ability to stick to an opponent like a magnet and follow his every move)

Ling kung jin (for hitting opponents without touching them).

Kua

Also Kwa. Variously referred to as the hips, pelvis, crotch, groin or more specifically as the hip crease, where the inside of your legs meet your torso, or the muscles around the hip joints.

Li

The power generated from muscular strength, as opposed to internal power, which does not use these muscles.

Qi

Intrinsic energy, vital substance, life force; the literal translation from Chinese is nearer to "breath" or "air". Qi is present in all living things but you cannot see or touch it.

Sifu

Combination of the characters "teacher" and "father". Traditionally, martial arts schools were viewed as an extended family, with each student designated younger or older brother, sister or uncle depending on their status.

In the West, we tend to translate the word as "master" as it implies that the person so-called has mastered their art and is fit to teach others. But it's not often used within Western tai chi schools, where we usually stick with "teacher" or "instructor" (the latter implying a lower level of qualification, usually denoting junior teachers within a large school).

Song

The state of relaxation in which tai chi should be performed. Completely relaxed, we would fall down, so we always maintain the low level bodily activity described as muscle tone. What we are looking for in tai chi is a partial contraction of the musculature, just enough to maintain equilibrium and upright posture.

Tui Shou

Otherwise known as push hands. Traditionally a two-person tai chi training routine in sensitivity and gaining a sense of engaging in combat. These days also a category in martial art competition.

Tu-na

"To utter and admit". A Taoist focused breathing exercise used in tai chi and qi gong.

Yi

The wisdom mind, that part which produces intention.

Yin & Yang

The two opposing but complementary forces which govern everything in nature. Yin is passive and negative force whilst Yang is active and positive. Yin-yang theory in China goes back thousands of years. The two forces are said to be in constant flux, and there is never a state of complete Yin or complete Yang, hence the symbol showing Yin (black) with a small area of Yang (white) and vice versa.

List of Chinese Characters

Anatomy

Many people find this a confusing subject. No wonder, as we have over seven hundred named muscles in our bodies, not to mention the muscle tissue found inside the heart, digestive organs, and blood vessels.

In order to benefit from the exercises in this book, you will need to know a little about how the body works and name some of its components. But a comprehensive knowledge is not necessary, and I've tried to keep references to anatomy simple, using terms which are in current usage where possible.

In the stretching section, when talking of areas with large and complicated muscle groups like the hips or shoulders, I have not gone into precisely which muscles are affected.

The following brief list expands upon the explanation of terms given in the book. If you are interested in finding more detailed information I would encourage you to consult a medical or anatomical text book.

Abductor

A muscle which draws a limb or body part away from the centre or another part.

Adductor

A muscle which draws a limb or body part towards the centre or another part.

Aerobic

Exercise which improves the heart and blood vessels' efficiency in absorbing and moving oxygen around the body.

Antagonistic

A muscle which opposes the action of another, one contracting whilst the other relaxes, for example the biceps and triceps.

Corset

The layers of muscle which wrap around the torso like an old-fashioned ladies' undergarment. They should contract with physical activity, protecting the internal organs from moving around.

Fascia

The tissue which surrounds all the muscles and organs of the body, forming sheets which connect and separate different parts. The structure of the fascial network is not constant, but rather changes with injuries or tensions, so that thick layers can appear, restricting movement. Until lately it was a relatively unexplored science in the West, but it has recently been proposed that the pathways correspond with the meridian lines and acupuncture points of Traditional Chinese Medicine (TCM).

Glutes

The three large muscles of the buttock, their full names are gluteus maximus (outer), gluteus medius (middle) and gluteus minimus (inner).

Hamstrings

A group of muscles situated at the back of the thighs, descending from the pelvis.

Hip Flexors

A flexor is a muscle which flexes a joint. The collective anatomical term for the hip flexors or inner hip muscles is iliopsoas and this comprises the psoas major (see below) and ilacus muscle.

Lactic Acid

An organic acid produced by the breakdown of glucose in the muscles during strenuous exercise.

Myotatic Reflex

The automatic contraction of muscles which prevents them from being stretched beyond their normal range.

Oblique Abdominals

These muscles run along the sides of the torso. They are used for rotation and inclination as well as stabilisation.

Pectorals

Two pairs of large muscles, pectoralis major and pectoralis minor, which connect the chest with the upper arms and shoulders.

Psoas

In this case the psoas major, situated at the base of the back or loin area and extending to the inner thigh (see Hip Flexors above). About 60% of people have a psoas minor muscle which, if present, helps to flex the hips.

Quads

The quadriceps muscles, four powerful muscles on the front of the thighs.

Rotator - external

Any muscle which rotates away from the centre of the body, found in the hips, knees, shoulders and eyeballs.

Rotator - internal

Muscles which rotate towards the centre of the body, found in the hips, knees, shoulders and eyeballs.

Sacrum

A triangular bone at the base of the spine comprising five fused vertebrae, which connects to the coccyx or tail-bone. The vertebrae are separate in children but will have joined together by the age of twenty six.

Scalenes

Scalenus muscles, three on each side of the neck running to the upper two ribs. They elevate the ribs and assist with neck movement and breathing.

Part 1 - Around Tai Chi

CHAPTER 1 – Tai Chi Tales

A more or less unbiased history of tai chi

Legend has it that a martial art resembling tai chi chuan was invented by Taoist monk Zhang Sanfeng. Many have tried to prove or disprove this theory, the lack of historical record presenting no obstacle. It is interesting to debate the possibilities, and tai chi practitioners often spend many hours engaged in this pastime. It's unlikely anyone will ever be able to come up with a categorical answer, so the debate will go on.

Read any book or article on tai chi and you'll find people relating diverse theories as if they were facts carved in stone by the first person ever to practise. Teachers too will often insist that there is only one way to do tai chi – theirs. Arguments are often based on the Tai Chi Classics, ancient writings on the basic principles to be followed. These can be difficult to understand, as they have been translated and interpreted many times over. Traditional Chinese characters are transformed into Simplified ones and the writings are then converted into English or another language, sometimes via English. They therefore tend to take on the theories and prejudices of the person who did the translation.

The nature of Chinese characters is rather different from that of words in English. Many are pictograms, stylised pictures of the words they represent. Also common is the ideograph, a simpler illustration of an idea, whilst the bulk of words combine one of the above with another element denoting the sound. Most words comprise two or more characters. The character "man" shown below comprises those for "field" and "strength".

In China, there are hundreds of dialects and some do not even have a written form. According to Ministry of Eduction figures, campaigns to improve literacy have raised the national rate from 20% in 1950 to over 85% in 2001.[2] To be able to read a newspaper, you'd need to know about 3,000 words, but there are actually over 100,000 in the Mandarin (official) tongue.

Martial arts in China were traditionally kept secret, with fathers even refusing to teach their daughters because they would eventually marry and disclose details to their husband's family. With only the elite able to read and write, and such arts being largely physical, it's not surprising that there aren't many historic records.

For qi gong, on the other hand, there are documents going back much further: over two thousand years. It is likely that tai chi has its origins in qi gong as well as other, so-called external martial arts such as those taught for centuries in the Shaolin Temple, a Buddhist monastery built in the 5th century following the introduction of Buddhism to China from India.

The Zhang Sanfeng story certainly lacks proof, whereas the other candidate for "Inventor of Tai Chi" has better documentation on his side. However, he lived considerably later and there is some doubt about his credentials too. A little "history" from both camps follows, starting with the colourful but inconsistent Zhang Sanfeng.

FOUNDERS OF TAI CHI CHUAN

Zhang Sanfeng was a Taoist monk, an immortal who lived for more than two hundred years (immortal – doesn't that mean he gets to live forever?) between midnight on 9th April 1247 and some time in the 15th century. Alternatively, he was born in 960 or 1279. Some say he was a big fat chap who didn't worry much about personal hygiene, others that he was small and very particular in his habits. Amongst the former it is said that he was at least seven foot tall. He could travel three hundred and fifty miles a day, though I can't say by what form of transport. He either saw or dreamed a crane fighting a snake and it was from this that the art of tai chi was born, the movements of his exercise system imitating that of either both combatants or just the snake.

When he wasn't wandering around China he lived at Wudang Mountain, where he created tai chi and taught it to the other inhabitants. Wudang has been a holy temple for around 1,300 years. By the alleged time of Zhang Sanfeng it was already a centre for Taoist and other learned practices including the study of TCM, meditation and qi gong. There is a statue of him there and those tai chi practitioners who consider him the founder of the art celebrate his birthday on the ninth day of the third month of the Chinese year.

Some say that Zhang Sanfeng was actually invented by Yang style proponents in the nineteenth century to counter the rising popularity of the Chen family and their assertion that their own style was the "Original Tai Chi".

Unsurprisingly, any history of tai chi chuan told by an exponent of the Chen style will assert that the art originated in the 17th century with the Chen family, in the Chen village, Chenjiagou, in Henan province, China. The accredited "inventor" was Chen Wangting, a former general in the army of the Ming Dynasty who was forced to retire when it was replaced by the Qing Dynasty.

However, it is also said that the practice was brought to Chen village by a second generation student of Zhang Sanfeng, a certain Jiang Fa. Apparently, the exercises being practised in the village were of such little use martially that he took pity on the family and taught them a proper fighting system, after first battering the lot in the manner of a kung fu movie circa 1970.

Jiang Fa may actually have taught the art in other villages, and in the spirit of tai chi legend, taught "The Real Thing", rather than the watered-down version he showed the Chen family. The Zaobao style in northern China claims to come from Jiang Fa and to pre-date Chen style, making it the "Original Tai Chi."

Jiang Fa's teacher was Wang Zongyue, first student of Zhang Sanfeng. Zongyue is thought to have built on the thirteen separate postures created by his teacher, turning them into a sequence, a forerunner of the forms we practise nowadays.

Zongyue is the ostensible author of the Salt Shop Manuals, writings which form part of the Tai Chi Classics. Some say that he, and not Zhang Sanfeng, was the true creator of the art and first person to employ the term "tai chi chuan" (but see below), as well as the famous statement: "A force of four ounces deflects 1,000 pounds." This principle is another subject for much pondering and dispute.

However, Zhang Sanfeng wrote his own treatise on tai chi, albeit not referring to it by that name. It is commonly considered to be the most important of the writings, apart from those of the Taoist sages, which while not strictly about tai chi, embody its principles (depending on which type of tai chi you do). There is no proof that he wrote it, of course, given that he may not even have existed.

Nevertheless, among other nuggets of wisdom Zhang stated that: "The root is at the feet, Jin generated from the legs, mastered by the waist and manifested from the fingers." Tai chi writings contain many references to something which is translated as the "waist". This has caused great confusion as Westerners struggle to understand which part of the body is actually being referred to. Prudishness among translators may account for a failure to substitute the pelvis, which makes a lot more sense.

Interestingly, most Wikipedia entries documenting the history of Yang style tai chi are prefaced with the caution "This article reads more like a story than an encyclopedia entry", whereas the Chen ones don't on the whole, giving them greater clout.

Turning now to the Chen family version of history, although it was Chen Wangting who invented tai chi, (see above) his ancestor Chen Bu had already established a martial arts school when he moved to and named Chenjiagou in 1374. (Commonly known as the Chen Village, the place name literally means something like "Chen family ditch" due to the area's topography). Wangting apparently incorporated daoyin qi gong and tu-na Taoist breathing techniques into the family style, techniques which had been around since 200BC. He also invented tui shou or push hands.

Wangting's creation took place during the Qing Dynasty (1644 – 1912) when China was ruled by invaders from Manchuria. It is recorded that in 1727 Manchu emperor Yongzheng banned the teaching of martial arts in China, nervous of his conquered subjects.

It is here that we begin to wonder about Wangting as a slight doubt enters along with a character called Jiang Fa. The two met whilst rebelling against the Qing empire. Jiang Fa was an officer with the insurgents and was forced to flee after the rebellion was unsuccessful. Starting what was to become something of a trend, he disguised himself as a servant and went to live in the Chen village. It is recorded that Chen Wangting called him his brother and acknowledged that he contributed to the creation of tai chi. How big was his contribution? Could he in fact have been the same Jiang Fa who studied under Zhang Sanfeng, or was that actually a clever story devised by Yang family supporters to throw doubt on Wangting's status and further muddy the tai chi waters?

THE YANG FAMILY

No one disputes that the creator of the Yang style of tai chi was Yang Luchan, although he was also known as Yang Fukui. He lived from 1799 to 1872 and came from a family of poor farmers. As a young man he studied martial arts including Chang Quan (long fist), a kung fu from Northern China which allegedly dates from the 10th century.

It seems strange that some Chinese martial arts claim to have a traceable history of hundreds of years whilst tai chi's is shrouded in mystery. Even Yang Luchan's martial studies are in question – another source says it was Shaolin boxing he studied.

Yang Luchan was a generally amiable character, except on a few notable occasions. Having worked undercover as a cleaner in the Chen family village, he was able to learn enough tai chi to impress the then head, Chen Chang Hsing, into letting him become the first student from outside the family.

Having spent eighteen years with the Chen family (or possibly only thirteen or even six), he began to travel widely, challenging anyone with a fierce reputation in any of the martial arts. He beat them all, without once injuring an opponent - not even accidentally. For his pains, he became known as Yang Wu Di – Yang The Invincible. During this time he perfected his own style of tai chi, which was derived from all that he had learned with the Chens and his experiences outside their village.

It is difficult to find out how Luchan changed and improved tai chi. Chen history claims that Yang style was mainly for fitness. Explosive force, deep postures, stamping and variations in tempo were taken out. He changed it because he had promised not to teach those outside Chenjiagou, and not in order to make it better. This begs the question how he could have ended up with his "Invincible" nickname and reputation.

In 1850, greatly impressed with his reputation, the Emperor of China called for Luchan to join the imperial bodyguard. The other guards were very jealous and hatched a plot to beat him to death whilst he lay sleeping on his first night in the palace. This they did and left poor Yang for dead. The next morning he was up and about, apparently none the worse for his midnight drubbing. However, none of the other guards turned up for duty, and on investigation were all found to have died from internal injuries. Presumably it was only with official challengers that Luchan applied his no-injuring rule.

Luchan became personal trainer to the other bodyguards (presumably a fresh batch) and also the Emperor's family members. The Manchu rulers were unpopular with the people of China and Luchan was reluctant to teach them his special art. In keeping with a tai chi tradition which continues to this day, he decided not to give away all his secrets to these outsiders, and in fact went to the extreme of taking out all the useful stuff. Thus was born the second Yang style. It is perhaps this version of Yang style tai chi to which Chen historians are referring. There is much debate over how much of the real Yang tai chi has survived to the present day.

Luchan fathered three sons, although one died in infancy. The others learned from their father and eventually became tai chi masters themselves. Luchan was said to be something of a tyrant - despite his gentleness with opponents - who forced his sons to work so hard that the younger, Yang Jianhou, repeatedly ran away, whilst his older brother, Yang Banhou, is alleged to have tried to hang himself. Luchan taught his sons both the authentic and the "new" or "Manchu" style, the latter having by this time become the official Yang family tai chi which was taught to their other pupils.

By all accounts, Banhou was a violent individual, often attacking his students and beating them brutally (perhaps something to do with his own experience at the hands of his father).

His brother Jianhou was said to be more gentlemanly and consequently had more students. It was he who first started teaching the private or original Yang style outside the family. He was the father of two sons, Yang Shaohou and Yang Chengfu. The elder son was adopted by Banhou and turned out to be even more fierce than his uncle. The younger, Chengfu, became the new face of tai chi, simplifying the form and allowing the art to become more accessible to all. Thus it began to spread around the world.

THE CHEN FAMILY

Back to the Chens, who in 1928 took their tai chi to Beijing. The style became very popular, as a result of Chen Zaope and his uncle Chen Fake's success against opponents of other arts martial. Some of his matches were held on a lei tai, or Striking Platform, a raised boxing ring without a railing popular in China since the 11th Century.

In olden times the platform was 2.5m high and combatants were often killed, either by falling off or because of the ferocity of the competitions. Nowadays there is a professionally recognised international Lei Tai Fighting art, but participants are well-protected, the platform has been lowered to 1.2m and the death toll has reduced considerably.

THE NAMING OF TAI CHI CHUAN

Chen Fake was apparently asked the name of his art, which was quite unlike anything seen in Beijing before, including the Yang style, now named tai chi chuan. His reply: "I don't know if it's tai chi chuan, I only practise my family's art," is oft-quoted in one of the other popular subjects for dispute: where did the current name originate?

Well, to begin with, what does it mean? The characters are translated as Supreme Ultimate Boxing or Fist. The Taiji (or tai chi, depending on your preferred system of pinyin) part refers to the great polarities in Taoism, represented by the taijitu symbol, commonly known as the Yin/Yang. The second part, chuan or quan, can be understood as "fighting system". The name is often misunderstood to mean that it is the most efficient fighting system ever invented, although it's difficult to imagine anyone winning a spontaneous fight using tai chi. All moves should be defensive – the tai chi practitioner never instigates but only responds to an attack. It is a defensive fighting system, always maintaining a balance and not going to extremes (a little yin within the yang and vice versa). Excessive force should never be employed, but rather a yielding and use of the opponent's own force against him.

Anyway, it seems that the Chens, alleged creators of tai chi chuan, didn't coin the term. Was it really Wang Zongyue, assuming he was a real person, or was it actually the founder of Yang style, the gentlemanly Yang Luchan? Wikipedia, again counselling a pinch of salt, states that Luchan's art was first known as Cotton Fist or Neutralising Fist, (Mien or Hua Quan). A scholarly spectator was moved by his performance in a match in Beijing and suggested that his techniques embodied the principles of Taoism. Thus, the name was born. The Chens subsequently decided to designate their own fighting system tai chi in order that it would be understood to be based on the same principles, albeit looking very different to the Yang style.

MORE HISTORY

Tai chi suffered a setback during the Chinese Cultural Revolution between the 1960s and 1970s when independent martial art schools were banned, along with many other educational activities. They were replaced by government controlled Wushu or Kuoshu (arts of the nation) schools which switched the emphasis from defence skills to sport or gymnastics. Tai chi went underground and resurfaced in China after Chairman Mao's death in 1976 when traditional teaching was again permitted during the Era of Reconstruction. But in the meantime many teachers had fled abroad, or been executed or otherwise discouraged from continuing their training.

In Chenjiagou, the standard had dropped and returning there in 1958 Chen Zaope was dismayed to find few skilled family members left, with the older members making no effort to pass their art on to the younger generation, who were ignorant and uninterested. He moved back to the village and started teaching, attempting to restore the standard of practice. However, his efforts were quickly thwarted by the 1966 prohibition.

As it happens, the Chen village had already survived a near crisis when Chen Fake, as a young boy, refused to apply himself and risked leaving the family without a skilled master. Fortunately, at fifteen he suddenly grew up (defying usual teenage behaviour) and started training really hard. He was said to do between thirty and one hundred forms per day, with pauses in which he snacked on a loaf of bread (he'd been a bit tubby in his pre-adolescent days).

Chen Fake turned out to be an exceptional tai chi master, introducing techniques better suited to combat, including more chansi (spiralling energy), fajing (explosive energy) and qinna (joint locking) with the creation of his new Xinjia form.

Many years earlier, Chen Changxing (1771-1853) had softened the form, which was becoming too demanding for older members of the family. He removed scissor kicks, jumps where one did a handstand or the splits on landing and a difficult move to envisage: the taking of a crouching stance then circling the head around the extended front leg. Changxing was known as "Mr Ancestral Tablet" for his upright stance, and one could speculate that it was he who found the movements too hard.

Some say the Chen tai chi taught now bears little resemblance to the original art. But then again, they probably practise Yang tai chi.

BACK TO THE FUTURE

The Five Mental Keys To Diligent Study, an anonymous treatise considered to be one of the Tai Chi Classics, states:

1. Study wide and deep
2. Investigate, ask
3. Ponder carefully
4. Clearly discriminate
5. Work perseveringly

Tai chi history is to some people a very serious matter, on which hinges the validity of their practice. I hope that my light-hearted look at the competing versions won't grievously offend those with strong views.

Too many people are happy to believe what they are told, and our confirmation bias   (a tendency to search for and interpret information which confirms what we already think) can stop us thinking openly and looking at things from all sides. It can be great fun debating the merits of different styles and likelihood of different versions of history, but it's best to stay light-hearted and balanced, keeping a sense of proportion.

Open your mind to the advantages of learning new skills; deviate from your path from time to time.

Tales From The Annals

QI GONG

Hundreds of push-ups, sit-ups and meditation are described as being preliminary methods to bring qi flow to a level high enough to commence training Iron Shirt, Iron Vest, Iron Palm and other appropriately named ways to improve strength and the ability to deliver and withstand blows. The actual techniques, described as "hard qi gong", include suspending heavy weights from the testicles (a master of the Testicle Eight Outstanding Techniques could drag a 500lb rock tied to his scrotum) and striking or slapping hard objects.

Mercifully, after such a work-out a traditional Chinese balm, Dit Da Jow, is applied. It is said that not applying the balm can lead to arthritis, stiffness or other nerve damage in the hands, as well as blindness brought on by clots in the blood vessels. Not doing the training could be another option...

APPLICATIONS

In martial arts, the form movements should always have a combat application which can be explained and demonstrated. Members of a karate school were fascinated with a particular kick, unable to decide what it meant. Eventually, they came to the conclusion that the master had been flicking his sandal off his foot and towards his opponent.

EQUINOPHOBIA

In 1925 Kuo Yu Chang, a master of Iron Palm and Iron Shirt, turned down the opportunity to make $1,000 worth of gold in return for the pleasure of smacking a horse. A Russian circus was offering this reward to anyone who could withstand three kicks from their horse.

Kuo took three kicks in the chest by the large animal, rested for half an hour, then returned and slapped it in the chest. The horse fell down dead from its internal injuries.

TRUTH OR LEGEND?

Many tales of martial arts stunts sound rather far-fetched, and these days it's very easy to fake a photo or video. But beware of doubting the verity of a real master. Shaolin abbot Hai Deng was well-known for his extraordinary feats, which included performing one fingered handstands despite being in his 70s.

A Hong Kong reporter scoffed at reports of his talents and following the abbot's death sued his estate for fraud. The court found that the handstand and other stories were true and ordered the chastened reporter to pay costs.

BEYOND THE GRAVE

In the preface to his book: Essence and Applications of Taijiquan[3], Yang Chengfu reminisces about learning from his grandfather, Yang Luchan. This is impressive, given the fact that he was born eleven years after Luchan's death. But then, tai chi is a very special art....

CHAPTER 2 – Internal Arts

QI GONG

Qi gong is the science of developing qi. For the purpose of this section, it's the practical activity of performing exercises to draw qi from outside and circulate it within our bodies.

Chinese people have been practising qi gong for thousands of years. There is evidence of this from scriptures, artwork and medical texts dating back over two thousand five hundred years. As well as physical exercises, the use of heat, massage, plants and tissue from living creatures were being used for healing. This tradition of Chinese medicine has continued ever since with much success and remarkably little change. In the West, we have made many advances, notably a very recent acceptance that TCM including acupuncture and acupressure is efficacious, sometimes more so than its Western equivalent.

So doctors in the West now sometimes use the two systems in tandem or interchangeably. They might also recommend that patients find a tai chi or qi gong class thereby taking joint responsibility for their own health.

Some people confuse tai chi and qi gong, and often both are taught within the same class. The word "chi" apparently appears in both, although in fact it has different meanings. The qi in qi gong is the one which stands for energy, whereas the other means "ultimate" (see Chapter 1 for a discussion of the name tai chi).

Some of the movements look similar to the untrained eye. However, whilst in qi gong you are often deliberately stretching to your limits, in tai chi movements should never extend beyond the natural. Arms are generally kept in front of your body as though you were holding a large ball. So qi gong can't be tai chi, but confusingly tai chi can be considered a type of qi gong if the movements are done slowly and with that intention. Qi gong is, after all, a far older art and they both involve the circulation of energy in the body.

The biggest visual distinction between qi gong and tai chi is that in the former you don't usually move your feet. This makes a huge difference to the ability of qi to circulate in the body. Whilst with tai chi and the other internal arts you are looking at a regime of many years' study before you start being able to feel and control qi as you practise your form, with a good qi gong teacher you could easily start having unusual bodily sensations within just a few sessions.

For this reason, it's ideal for those less able or willing to devote large chunks of their lives to the practice. The forms are also much easier to remember and there's no need for exceptional levels of flexibility and mobility (although they'll still help). It is said that even doing an approximation of form movements will have physical benefits. These could be limited to those experienced by getting out of the house and not sitting in an armchair all evening, of course.

Qi gong is credited with the same health benefits as tai chi. There are specific forms for the internal organs as categorised by TCM (not the same as in Western medicine), and doing them regularly has been found to promote good all round health as well as helping with specific issues.

Many people use qi gong to complement their tai chi and develop attributes which will be useful in their practice. For example, the ancient form Yijin Jing is known throughout the world and has been used in the Shaolin Temple for 1,500 years. It is said that the Bodhidarma brought it to the temple in the fifth century from India and trained monks to perform the exercises to counter the effects of hours spent in seated meditation.

A rather more prosaic version of its history has the form coming from the countryside: farmers used it to help them do their heavy manual work.

The name is translated as Muscle/Tendon Changing Classic Qigong and it is one of the more physical forms. By strengthening the muscles and tendons, the exercises improve speed, flexibility, balance and coordination. As with most qi gong (the "Iron" versions excepted!) they can be done more or less whole-heartedly but to achieve these goals the body needs to be stretched to its limits, with the spine turning and bending in several movements. The form claims to target the twelve meridians specified in TCM and the corresponding internal organs.

There are estimated to be many thousands of qi gong forms around and many different ways of categorising them. They include seated and lying forms (very useful for the elderly, convalescents and those with other health problems or reduced mobility). Some involve self-massage and sexual qi gong either alone or with a partner is also popular. Motivation normally falls in the categories martial, medical and spiritual.

Tai Chi Styles

We have already seen how complicated the history of tai chi is. Traditionally, books would state that there were five main schools each carrying the family name of its creator. These were: Chen, Yang, Wu, Sun and Wu Hao. Nowadays, you are unlikely to find a Wu Hao school outside China but there's a good chance you'll locate a school with a completely new name. Enquire and you will often find that it is a descendent of one of the original five.

Another phenomenon is that of the "Secret Style", only recently discovered or previously kept strictly for "Number One" disciples. The Yang Family Snake Style is said to be one such, although some people claim it is a recent creation. To confuse matters there are several other snake or serpent tai chi and kung fu styles in existence.

Any tai chi style should embody the basic principles including circular flowing movements, relaxed posture with body in alignment and a concentrated mind.

CHENG MANCHING

One example of a new designation for a tai chi with old origins is that of Cheng Manching, one time pupil of Yang Chengfu. The style has become known as Cheng Tai Chi as it has grown in popularity. This may cause some confusion with Chen Tai Chi (also known as Tai Chi Chen) for the uninitiated. The style is described as a lazy version of Yang, with the body less erect and the number of postures in the standard form reduced from eighty five or one hundred and eight (depending on how you count them) to a mere thirty seven.

WUDANG

Another newcomer is Wudang Tai Chi Chuan (Also known as Practical Tai Chi Chuan). This doesn't come from Wudang, but rather from Hong Kong. It too has its roots in Yang style tai chi but also claims links with the Chen and Wu styles. The name was apparently chosen to honour Wudang monk Zhang Sanfeng as creator of tai chi (see Chapter 1).

Practitioners often wear rather striking black and white costumes comprising a long tunic with slits up the sides, leggings and kung fu slippers with round openings in the sides.

CHEN

Despite being, to many people, the Original One True Tai Chi, this style is much less popular than Yang. This may be due to its lower stances, explosive movements and general reputation as a more martial version of the art.

However, many schools, especially in Asia, will teach both Chen and Yang styles side by side. It is said to be a good idea to study a "softer" style such as Yang or Sun before embarking on the Chen style, otherwise your tai chi may become hard and external, more like kung fu.

YANG

Yang is the most widespread of the styles, in part due to the Chinese government's commissioning of the Simplified 24 Step Form. The theory is that you can go to a class anywhere in the world and learn the same form. There are often exhibitions of this form involving large numbers of people. One of the most notable, involving over a thousand performers, was held by the Chinese in Tiananmen Square in 2008.

WU

This style was created by Wu Chuan Yau, a pupil of both Yang Luchan and his son Yang Banhou. It is said that he learned both the softer, "Manchu" style and the authentic version of Yang style tai chi, one of the rare outsiders to be so privileged. He then created his own style, opened a school and began teaching common people rather than only the elevated royal family and their employees.

The feet are generally kept closer together than in Yang and Chen styles, and this makes it a good option for those with existing knee problems, as the legs are under less stress. Movements are noticeably smaller. The form movements are said to be easier to learn, leaving practitioners with more freedom to concentrate on internal feelings.

The style also includes training in push hands and sparring and even has a wheelchair form.

WU HAO

Also called Wu (Hao), this style was created by Wu Yu Xiang and his nephew Li Yi Yu, and further developed by their student Hao Wei Zheng. Wu Yu Xiang studied with both Yang Luchan and Chen Chinping. He was also a student of Confucianism, Taoism and warcraft. The alleged treatise of Wang Zongyue, part of the Tai Chi Classics, was apparently found by his family in a Beijing salt shop and this he studied as well.

Steps are small and circular, stance high and the movements very compact. Each hand always protects its own side of the body. It is said to be a very internal style. Whilst it is popular in China, you will probably struggle to find a class in the West.

SUN

Sun style is the newest of the five original family styles. Its creator was Sun Lutang, an expert in Baguazhan and Xingyiquan already before he started studying tai chi with the Wu Hao family. Lutang was a Taoist and scholar whose writings about the internal arts are highly regarded. He was also the first person to write about there being two distinct styles of martial art: internal and external.

Another first was his inclusion of women as students. His daughter, Sun Jianyun, became a tai chi master and national martial arts judge as well as the creator of several tai chi forms and author of numerous books and videos on the subject. She died in 2003.

Sun tai chi has a style of stepping noticeably different from the others. As each foot steps, forward or backwards, the other follows it. The movements seem thus more agile and one can easily imagine that the response to an opponent's moves would be quicker and more effective.

The movements are comparatively small and stances high. There is a strong emphasis on opening and closing in the forms. In keeping with Sun Lutang's background, elements of Bagua and Xingyi can be seen in the footwork and postures.

The style's reputation for concentrating strongly on internal work as well as being less physical than Yang and Chen, makes it popular with students whose primary goals are overall health or the study of internal energy.

Other Internal Arts

BAGUAZHANG

As with tai chi, there are various theories surrounding the origin of Bagua (as it is usually known).

The most convincing seems to be that it was created some time in the nineteenth century by Dong Haichuan, a martial artist and Taoist who combined walking meditation practice with his more physical skills. The result was the "circle walking" which is the most striking aspect of the art.

Practitioners maintain constant movement with direction changes combined with defensive body and arm movements. It is considered to be a very effective martial art, as the opponent is disorientated and confronted from unexpected angles.

Bagua is considered a useful skill for security professionals and often included in training for bodyguards, which doesn't tend to be the case with tai chi.

It's popular with a variety of students for all the same reasons as the latter, including self-defence, general health, fitness, meditation and spirituality. Classes with these different features emphasised are held all over the World.

XINGYIQUAN

Xingyi (as it is commonly called), is described as an "aggressive" art with attacks in a straight line. It is alleged to have been created by Yue Fei, a famous twelfth century Chinese general, but this is probably not true. Once again there is no evidence for the claim. It may perhaps be the brainchild of Ji Long Feng, a celebrated swordsman who is recorded as teaching the art around 1600.

The linear movements and emphasis on striking make it a surprise candidate for the common grouping with tai chi. However, it is said to be of Taoist origin and internal health and power are important aspects of training, with standing meditation a common practice.

Xingyi is often studied by bodyguards and others in the security profession. It is said to raise the spirit so that practitioners will be brave but calm and in control. The forms are said to be relatively simple to learn, and better health, strength, fitness, balance and coordination are among the claimed benefits.

CHAPTER 3 – Tai Chi Bonuses

The number and variety of benefits it is claimed that one can get from doing tai chi is quite surprising and it is tempting to dismiss some of the claims. But when I gave a little thought to how it had benefited me, aside from my enjoyment of and improvement in the actual practice itself, I quickly produced the following list:

- coordination
- flexibility
- mobility
- circulation
- endurance
- muscular strength
- pelvic floor function
- immunity
- digestion
- eyesight
- deceleration of ageing process
- aerobic capacity
- dancing
- swimming
- making friends
- sexual enjoyment
- relationships

- body shape
- self-confidence
- sleep
- ability to relax
- calmness
- less stress
- breathing
- sensitivity
- patience
- perception
- reasoning
- memory
- concentration
- mindfulness
- determination

Yes, I know that's quite a substantial list. Put another way, I have gained mentally, physically, emotionally and spiritually. Or yet another, I feel smarter, happier and healthier.

A lot of the benefits haven't directly come from the tai chi, but rather the various activities around tai chi which have become part of my practice and which are included in this book. They didn't all come at once and many are still ongoing. For example, I continue to work on deepening my breathing which makes my immune system, circulation, digestion, sleep and other functions better and better. Relaxation can be a frustrating process, as the more relaxed you are, the more you notice the bits that still need a lot of work. But although there may be setbacks and injuries, everything is constantly moving in a positive direction.

Spatial Awareness

A simple definition of spatial awareness is the ability to consciously understand the relationship in space between oneself and surrounding structures and objects. But it's more than that. It encompasses such matters as knowing roughly what time of day it is, finding our way and having a feel for the amount of personal space most people find acceptable.

This is something we start to learn in childhood, often aided by lessons in school designed for the purpose. Young children lack awareness of their own body, but with time should gain this ability, helped by participation in playing games and sports. In adolescence it can deteriorate, as we grow too quickly to comprehend the limits of our physical body. Teenagers commonly grow extremely quickly - boys as much as 9cm and girls 8cm per year - and in consequence the centre of gravity lifts, causing balance problems as the brain struggles to catch up. Once this settles down we go to work. Traditionally this involved physical activity for most people, which would help us regain and retain our spatial awareness until in old age we start to lose it, as our senses begin to decline.

In the past one hundred years work has become much more sedentary. Even formerly physical jobs such as farming have become mechanised. The games children play commonly involve much less movement and lots of us spend more hours watching the television or computer than doing anything vaguely energetic. Thus there are fewer physically active people of all ages and consequently a general diminution in spatial awareness. The effects of this include an increase in accidents and their severity.

Doing tai chi brings a natural improvement in spatial awareness, heightening as it does our interior and exterior awareness. This makes practitioners less prone to and also less affected by accidents, as we are often able to minimise the impact. Being able to relax makes the effects of falls less severe and we can better withstand an impact such as a car crash. A tense body will always suffer more serious injury, which is why sleeping or otherwise unconscious victims often come off more lightly in an accident.

Interactions

Apart from the myriad benefits I've already mentioned, the emotional sensitivity tai chi seems to bring can be of great help in any situation where you are called upon to communicate with others. Practitioners often report that they become more sensitive to other people's feelings and better able to judge how to tackle difficult situations. Tai chi skills include a variety of "jins" or energies useful for different purposes.

I have a friend who works in the construction industry, where he is called upon to negotiate on and off site with others involved in the projects at all levels. Circumstances are often highly charged and stressful. He tells me that since he's being doing tai chi, interactions are much more easily managed. It goes something like this:

Your listening energy (ting jin) makes you more sensitive to the mood of your colleagues. Your understanding energy (dong jin) allows you to sense the direction of a problem and discern the reasons behind it. You can remain impartial and thus help to resolve issues that arise. You will be able to neutralise a situation with delicacy, good timing and an appreciation of the angles or different viewpoints involved. (Neutralising energy or hua jin.) Finally, you will be better able to focus your efforts, instinctively making the right decisions. (Discharging energy or fa jin.)

The same formula can be applied to all your interactions, with friends, family or passing acquaintances. You may find that your new more open posture and habit of looking up and around you will attract people to you and you'll engage in brief but rewarding conversations or the exchange of smiles.

The world can be a much friendlier place than we make it when we're locked into our negative thoughts, self-absorption and obsession with the next thing. Live in the moment; revel in your supple body and lively mind. Keep doing tai chi.

Diverse Talents

People who play sports, dance or have some other hobby involving physical activity will usually have an innate advantage in the tai chi class. You'll have seen them: those annoying folk who seem to have mastered in a few weeks what you've been struggling with for a year!

But take heart. It's often those who find tai chi the most difficult who will be the ones to stick with and get the most benefits from it in the end. There is more satisfaction in doing something well if you've found it really difficult. Also, having spent a lot of time learning something and exploring the mechanics more deeply, you may find it stays fixed in your mind, whereas a lesson quickly mastered is often just as quickly forgotten.

These slow learners are likely to make the best future teachers, too, because having had difficulties themselves, they know what others are likely to find hard.

A teacher who has never experienced rigid hips, lack of balance or problems remembering the movements can only approach these issues theoretically and may have difficulty empathising or finding a way to help students overcome such impediments to practising tai chi. But if you've struggled yourself you can relate to those who are in the same situation.

CHAPTER 4 – Tai Chi Training

Beginning Tai Chi

The exact origin of tai chi as an exercise is extremely hazy, but it's true to say that similar activities have been around for hundreds of years and were first practised in Chinese monasteries. At its core is the principle of mind and body as a unit, harmonising with the natural world. It is associated with both Chinese philosophy and TCM. It is a martial art but one used passively rather than aggressively. It emphasises the development and movement of qi within the body which is said to improve health and allow practitioners to defend themselves without the use of muscular strength. It is used as a meditation and means to spiritual growth.

So that, very briefly, is traditional tai chi. But the chances are you'll encounter something rather less ethereal if you take up tai chi in the West during the 21st century. It is claimed by some that the "true" or "temple" tai chi hasn't been taught since the revolution of 1900-1910, and by others that it was lost in Mao's Cultural Revolution of 1966-76.

Certainly, little of the tai chi now taught appears to have retained the essence of the legendary art. Concentration is generally on correct performance of the movements of forms which themselves been simplified to have mass appeal.

However, most of us aren't able or willing to devote ourselves to months of standing and walking practice before we even start to learn the first movement, or to allow tai chi to dominate our lives completely. Therefore, a tai chi which is accessible to all is far more appropriate for the modern world. These days there are a variety of reasons for starting tai chi and I've discussed some of the most common below. It's likely that more than one will be involved, and I'm sure there are plenty I haven't mentioned.

Health professionals are increasingly likely to recommend tai chi (or qi gong) as a slow and gentle exercise which is suitable for just about everyone, whatever their situation. Thus its popularity is growing and the variety of styles and emphasis mean that, at least if you're in a city or prepared to travel, you should be able to find something which dovetails with your objectives.

Some teachers will let you try a class for free although others seem to actively discourage new members. Don't be offended if this happens – it's usually because the class is well-established and students are at about the same level. Instructors feel they can't devote the necessary time to beginners without disrupting the harmony of the group.

Many get round this by holding separate classes for different levels or allowing their senior students to help with teaching. The latter is a good method of enabling the seniors to progress within the school under the supervision of their teacher.

Why Tai Chi?

◆ **Physical Health**

According to various studies, doing tai chi can improve physical functioning and quality of life in conditions including arthritis, stroke, Parkinson's Disease, heart conditions and cancer. It is also said to help maintain bone density, which is often an issue for post-menopausal women, and to reduce blood pressure.

◆ **Mental Health**

Tai chi is cited as improving psychological health by alleviating stress, anxiety and depression, improving general mood and increasing self-esteem.

◆ **Self-defence**

Tai chi is first and foremost a martial art. You practise defence skills at a slow pace, which allows for a smooth application when you're called upon to use them at speed. Increased confidence will also make you less likely to be a victim, as potential attackers often prey on those who appear frightened.

◆ **Social Interactions**

Attending a regular exercise class is a great way to meet people. One of the first things I noticed about doing tai chi was the way in which it enriched my social life. I often found that I had views and tastes in common with other attendees and I have made some good friends around the world.

◆ **Style**

There are several different styles of tai chi, and you may feel drawn to a particular one, for instance Chen because it's the oldest, Yang the most widely practised or Sun because the stepping's really nice. But as a beginner it will be hard to decide which suits you best and rapport with your teacher and the group, as well as the more mundane considerations of location and time, are also important. If you can try a few classes before deciding on one, do so. It's rarely a good idea to do more than one style at the same time until you've been practising for several years.

◆ **Push Hands**

Push hands has become something of a stand-alone practice for some. I know several teachers who concentrate far more on this aspect than solo tai chi form. Conversely, there are many schools where push hands is not practised at all.

- **Martial**

Tai chi remains a martial art, despite the trend towards focusing on its health benefits, and many schools' disregard for applications or partner work. Those who take up tai chi as a martial art train with this aspect in mind and enjoy discovering the ways in which the movements can be used to foil an attack. It is said that you should try to find at least three applications for each posture: striking, controlling the partner's joints and a defensive block. The skills taught in classes which focus strongly on the martial side may seem more akin to external kung fu than the soft internal power of tai chi.

- **Gymnastics**

Some would argue that the modern forms, created in China since the 1950s with the idea of making tai chi accessible to all, are effectively gymnastics. They are often practised with great attention to exact positioning and little to martial application or internal feelings.

- **Dance**

Lots of people are attracted by the beauty and grace of the form movements, and see tai chi as a dance, with a choreographed routine performed in harmony by the whole class. If ever you practise tai chi outside, chances are someone will come along and say it looks beautiful. Unless you're in China, in which case they'll tell you you're doing it all wrong.

◆ **Competitions**

There is a large faction of tai chi practitioners who are very competitive, and no shortage of international competitions in form and push hands. This side of the art often appeals to younger people and thus gives it a wider demographic.

◆ **Internal Energy**

Feeling your qi. Internal martial arts claim to use it to power their movements, rather than li (muscular force). In true tai chi, the form is not a direct action performed deliberately but rather results from the use of the yi (mind) to lead the qi with the body making the moves involuntarily. This is a difficult concept to grasp, but it's a fundamental element of ancient tai chi and something serious students will eventually wish to pursue.

◆ **Meditation**

Tai chi is regularly referred to as a "moving meditation". To begin with, it's likely to be more an exercise in concentration and mindfulness, both skills for meditation. But for many years there are so many things to think about: remembering the movements, having the body correctly aligned, the sense of an opponent, breathing, that you can't really consider it to be such. However, as you become more advanced you may be able to enter a meditative state as you practise. Indeed, meditation will be necessary if you wish to become acquainted with your qi.

◆ **Spirituality**

Hand in hand with meditation goes the spiritual side of tai chi. Developing the ability to move naturally with greater awareness of your body can lead to a feeling of connection with nature and a sense that you are a part of a greater whole.

◆ **Philosophy**

Tai chi was born out of Taoism, embodying its principles such as yielding, softness, being centred, balance and pragmatism. Yin and Yang theory is crucial both to the Taoist philosophy and an understanding of the mechanism of tai chi. Ancient Taoist writings are often consulted: there is a tradition of association between the I Ching and the positions of tai chi and many people look to the Tao Te Ching for guidance in its execution.

Personally, I always find it hard to answer when asked why I do tai chi. I have already explained that fear of ageing drew me to it, and that is certainly true, although as long as I can remember I hankered after learning a martial art, initially one of the external ones with lots of kicking.

For whatever reason I didn't act on this desire until I was in my late thirties, which was partly why I gravitated towards the relatively sedate tai chi.

Since then I've found my views and motivation shift regularly, and that's probably the key to my interest. There are so many layers and levels on which to view it that one can never get to the core, never stop learning and never get bored.

As well as going to regular classes, there are often opportunities to attend relatively inexpensive occasional events. Residential workshops in the UK and Europe are a great way to meet folk from other regions and countries, as well as to try out different styles of tai chi, push hands, the other internal Chinese arts or qi gong.

The number of styles available these days seems to be growing, paradoxically for an ancient art. Apparently some have been "hidden" until very recently. Such claims should probably be viewed with a dollop of scepticism.

Studying Abroad

Many schools run trips to China and will deal with the bureaucracy and paperwork for you. These usually combine a bit of sightseeing with some days spent training at a tai chi school, often that with which the Western school is affiliated. Some people find that they don't have enough time to get more than a taste for either the many sights or the training, but it is a relatively painless way to visit the birthplace of tai chi.

You could also consider studying abroad full time. Accommodation, food and tuition are all relatively affordable for Westerners, and it's an opportunity to really devote time to your tai chi which may be impossible at home.

Thailand

An option which could be taken as an extended holiday is to study in Lumphini Park, Bangkok, Thailand's home of tai chi. There are many groups which you can join for a shorter or longer period of time. Typically, it costs less than £10 per month for a two hour session every day from 7am to 9am, and you may be able to try a couple free of charge.

Usually there are some English speakers and local instruction, supplemented by a Chinese master who visits for a few weeks once a year. Most are practising Yang style tai chi, hand and weapon forms, but there is also qi gong and Bagua and even a Wu Hao group. You should bear in mind that they often comprise a group of enthusiasts of greater or lesser ability and operate as members' clubs rather than formal classes. If you attend during the master's visit you will be expected to contribute towards his fee.

The park comes to life at 4.30am, by which time there are already stalls lining the fences and a food court inside which serves a variety of cheap Thai meals. There's a vegetarian restaurant offering Khao Tom (rice soup) as well as lots of other rice and noodle options and a remarkable variety of soya products. The food court is closed and deserted by 10am, a source of some bemusement to late-rising tourists.

By 5am many of the classes are already in progress, or people have gathered to start practising. There are also a lot of joggers who circle the park. Lumphini is a 142 acre oasis in a heavily populated city, with a small island, interesting structures such as the Chinese Pavilion and two lakes with pedal boats for hire. There's a jogging track, a number of outdoor gyms as well as a swimming pool and sports centre (members only).

The park boasts a resident population of cats, dogs, birds, turtles and monitor lizards all apparently living in harmony. During the day it's quiet, but early in the morning hundreds of people come regularly to socialise and improve their health.

China

Another alternative is to study at a tai chi school in China, and this is what I did when I first visited the country. Residential courses start from about £550 per month. Locations to consider include Chen Jia Gou (the Chen Village), Xian, Wudang Mountain and Yangshuo (Guilin).

The standard of accommodation and teaching is extraordinarily variable, and it is not uncommon to find that the "master" is not in residence and all instruction will be carried out by his or her senior students.

My own experience was in Yangshuo, where I signed up for a month's tuition in Yang and Chen styles at a non-residential school. As seems to happen quite often, the school's website gave highly inaccurate information ranging from exaggerations to real whoppers. The teacher spoke about ten words of English, and as my Chinese was at about the same level communication was somewhat difficult.

After the month I switched to another teacher, which happily turned out very well. However, had I not been in China already I would have been unable to find him, as he has no premises and doesn't advertise. He was recommended by another Western student and all our lessons were held in the local park, (where locals often came to watch, comment and even join in at times).

Although learning tai chi in this way can be a really memorable experience, I would caution you to be wary. The Chinese are a very enterprising people, and tai chi schools for foreigners something of a growth industry. Before committing yourself, consider the following:

- **Training schedule**

  How many hours will you train, and in what disciplines? (Form, qi gong, stretching, internal exercises.) What tuition will be conducted by the Sifu or master himself?

- **School and teachers' credentials**

  Not easy to divine. If possible consult former students or a website such as The China Tai Chi Guide.[4] Look at what the school claims about lineage. Google them – dissatisfied students often speak out on the internet.

- **Access to English speakers**

  It's important that the teacher(s) can explain what they're teaching verbally and even a good translator is not ideal compared with being able to communicate directly. Outside class, you will want to be able to raise any concerns or ask questions of someone with authority within the school.

- **School size & other students**

How many pupils are there? What's the ratio of teachers to pupils? Which countries do the others come from? How long are they staying?

- **Level of instruction**

What experience do you have already? How is your fitness? Are the courses advertised at an appropriate level for you?

- **Style and forms taught**

Is this what you're interested in learning? If you're only going for a couple of months a long form may not be the best choice.

- **Assistance with visa**

Chinese visas are a bureaucratic nightmare and often involve travelling to another city once a month (or even another country) then waiting for a few days for a new one to be issued. Lots of paperwork will be required and the authorities often seem to think up new requirements on the spot. It's much less painful if the school can help out, starting with the initial visa before you leave home.

- **Premises**

These vary greatly and not all have covered teaching areas. If you are going in winter, or somewhere with a lot of rain, you'll want the building to be fairly substantial. Is there a place you can practice out-with lesson times?

- **Standard of accommodation**

Again variable, and they can be quite Spartan. The Chinese are much tougher than we Westerners and heating, hot water and even throne toilets are considered luxuries in many places. The beds are often akin to divans with no mattress.

- **Food**

If you have any special dietary requirements be aware that they are unlikely to be catered for. (I found being a vegetarian to be quite a challenge in China.)

- **Help with local interactions**

Does the school offer some kind of induction to the local shops, restaurants and transport arrangements? This is especially important if it is not residential.

◆ **Transport**

Will the school send someone to collect you from the airport or station? Even if you speak Mandarin interactions with locals can be very difficult, and in many cities there will be a line of people waiting to try to trick and rip you off.

◆ **Amenities**

Are there any local amenities such as a park, cinema or public swimming pool? In many parts of China the park is a focal point for social activity with groups meeting to gamble or practise dancing, tai chi and qi gong. Foreigners are normally welcome to join in – though you may find yourself the object of intense observation and amusement.

◆ **Environment**

Check this out before deciding where to go. Many Chinese cities are a bit grim, with serious pollution and permanent traffic jams. Northern China is worse than the south, with Xian and most of Hebei province boasting appalling air quality. In 2013 none of the seventy four Chinese cities examined for a World Health Organisation report met their recommendations.[5] Season is important, with spring and autumn generally being the times of least pollution.

◆ **Climate**

> China is subject to seasons not unlike Europe and a temperate climate which often means it's damp and cool. It can also be extremely hot and humid, especially in the south. Winters are pretty unpleasant in southern provinces which are ill-equipped for colder weather. This is typically addressed by donning thermal underwear, padded jackets and lined rubber boots, worn indoors in the absence of building insulation or central heating.

Even whilst writing this list, I know that it would be next to impossible to gather all this information in advance. Having blithely departed for China without any of it - the few things I thought I knew turned out to be incorrect - I still managed to get by, and stayed for four months on the first occasion. But I hope it gives you some ideas to think about before setting out on your adventure.

Chinese people can be very kind and someone with a little English will usually turn up to help you, though sometimes it's hard to tell the difference between the helpers and the tricksters. Be patient, don't panic and go with your tai chi developed instincts.

Part 2 – Exercising

CHAPTER 5 – Exercise Tips

Routine

Ideally you'll exercise every day. There's no need for a rest day with this type of activity, although other commitments may force you to take the odd day off. In order to see tangible changes in your flexibility you should be doing the stretches daily. Even then, you probably won't see much benefit for a few months, but if you were an impatient sort of person you wouldn't be practising tai chi.

Once you're familiar with all the exercises in this book, you may want to design a programme taking into account the time available and areas on which you feel you need to concentrate most. Be realistic about when and for how long you will be able to exercise. First thing in the morning is often the best time, before you've had a chance to talk yourself out of it or events have conspired against you.

Tai chi itself is traditionally practised at dawn and dusk when the earth's yin and yang energies are in balance. Some people find that the phases of the moon have an effect on their practice.

I recommend doing the exercises which you find the most difficult or unpleasant first; if you don't you may well find you conveniently haven't left enough time for them. Also, begin by exercising the side of your body which is less supple. Most people will find that their dominant side is stronger but less flexible than the other. As you become better acquainted with your body, you will be aware of areas where this is the case, and can work on trying to achieve an overall balance.

Number of Repetitions

For repeated exercises, you may notice that I have often suggested doing nine or eighteen repetitions. Qi gong form movements are often done nine times, and it is a very significant number in Taoist philosophy. It is the highest integer, containing all the other numbers, symbolises the fusion of yin and yang, and is the number of heaven. It is said that the body has nine openings: eyes, ears, nostrils, mouth, anus and either the urethra or the sexual organ. (If you count both women turn out to have ten which rather spoils things.)

In any event, nine (shown above) is important and it is thought that performing movements in multiples of nine builds qi. I don't have any proof that it works, but it does no harm to try.

The Chinese believe strongly in the significance of numbers. Three, five, seven, eight and nine are all considered lucky, though conversely five may be unlucky in combination with other numbers. Four is always unlucky, as the sound is very like that for "death". Chinese buildings often have no fourth floor and telephone numbers which include the digit are unpopular.

Water

Along with stretching, being properly hydrated increases flexibility as water lubricates the joints and cartilages enabling them to move more freely. It helps flush out toxins and distributes blood plasma, oxygen, minerals, and nutrients around the body. Dehydration is a common cause of headaches and lack of energy.

The European Food Safety Authority currently recommends a water intake of 2 litres per day for women and 2.5 litres for men.[6] This includes water within other beverages and food. Need varies according to personal size, activity level and temperature, though, and there's no hard and fast rule for everyone. It's very difficult to consume too much water, and you should definitely drink more when you're exercising.

Clothes

One of the great things about tai chi is that you don't need any special equipment or clothing (despite the fact that there's lots available). The same goes for the exercises in this book. You will find a few small accessories mentioned, which are inexpensive and widely available. The main thing is to wear comfortable, loose clothing, preferably made from natural materials. For the breathing exercises in particular I'd recommend removing bra and belt. You can wear your tai chi shoes (flat and flexible-soled or kung fu slippers) or go barefoot. T-shirts should have plenty of room around the armpits and not be low cut if there's any chance you'll have an audience. Trousers with a low crotch are best, especially for the leg stretches, otherwise they'll cut into your kua.

Health

If you are unwell or injured, it's not a good idea to just carry on regardless, but on the other hand there may be exercises which you can continue to do and which might even help you feel better. For example, I find that a headache vanishes for the duration of my tai chi practice, although it may well return straight afterwards. Pulled muscles or other injuries should be treated with caution, and may need to be rested, but you can still exercise the other parts of your body.

CHAPTER 6 – Warm Up

It's not a good idea to start doing tai chi "cold". However, the problem with most tai chi warm-up routines is that they are high energy and have the effect of heating and strengthening the muscles.

Whilst this is desirable for aerobic exercise including most martial arts, in tai chi, the movement is slow, its intensity comparable to a moderately paced walk. It is therefore not necessary to warm the muscles, but rather to increase their suppleness. The warm-up should also serve to get the blood flowing and open up the joints.

Before your tai chi practice, use these exercises to loosen your neck, wrists, elbows, shoulders, spine, hips, knees and ankles and finish with a whole body movement. They are all slow paced movements with a good range designed to open the body in readiness for tai chi, rather than to build up strength. Most of them came from my teacher in China.

Notes on the Warm Up

All exercises start with feet a little more than shoulder width apart, legs straight but not tensed, knees very slightly bent. Your arms and shoulders should be relaxed. Keep a space about the size of a small orange in each armpit. Unless otherwise instructed, start with eighteen repetitions each side for each exercise.

The complete routine should take ten minutes or so. Once you are familiar with the exercises and more aware of your body, you will want to adjust this, spending more time on areas which you feel are tense.

The Exercises

Neck Stretch

Breathe in and move your neck slowly to the side, keeping your chin tucked in and your shoulders relaxed. When you have turned as far as is comfortable, breathe out whilst returning your head to the centre. Try to feel the elastic-like stretch and release as your neck reaches its furthest point.

Wrist Roll

Link your fingers and hold your arms out in front of you at chest level. Roll wrists towards you in turn, eighteen times each side, then roll outwards, again eighteen times each side.

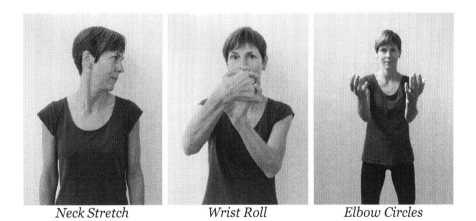

Neck Stretch　　　*Wrist Roll*　　　*Elbow Circles*

Elbow Circles

Hold your arms out at shoulder height, forming a curve in front of your body with palms facing down. Bring the arms together and when they are almost touching from elbows to fingers, pull your hands towards your chest, then round and out on each side to form two circles, finishing in the starting position.

Shoulder Opening

Raise your arms to shoulder height, but this time bring your shoulder blades back without lifting the tops of your shoulders or your scalenes (the muscles just above your collarbone which connect to your upper ribs).

Form loose fists and move arms in a circular motion until your hands come together, then out in a slightly larger circle with fingers extended.

Keep making alternate sized circles, bring your arms back to the starting position each time. Try to feel the elasticity in your joints as the arms stretch forward, rather like a swimming motion.

Shoulder Opening 1   *Shoulder Opening 2*

Spine Rotation

Hold arms out at shoulder height, in a natural position in front of your chest with palms facing down and elbows slightly lower than your hands. Keep hands in this position as you use your waist to move your upper body slowly to one side as far as it will comfortably go. Your knees should stay facing straight forward.

As you reach your limit at one side, you should feel your muscles extend like a elastic band; relax your hips and you return automatically to the centre. Move to the same side again, return to centre then repeat on the other side.

Spine Rotation 1

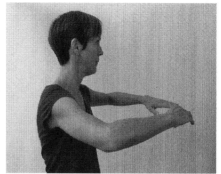
Spine Rotation 2

Spine With Loose Arms

Continue to move from side to side with knees facing ahead but now let your arms go. The motion will impel them across your body, hitting you somewhere on your back, shoulders and upper arms. Don't force this, allow the arms to move naturally and freely.

Hip Rocking

Take a forward stance, feet still shoulder width apart, one leg forward with knee bent, shin vertical, the other leg straight but not locked. Now move your weight slowly back and forth from foot to foot, trying to feel the point where your weight naturally wants to return to the other leg. Make sure your knees don't turn inwards. Repeat with other leg forward.

Spine, Loose Arms 1 *Spine, Loose Arms 2* *Hip Rocking*

Hip Circles

Circle your hips horizontally by moving your weight from one foot to the other. As you circle your balance shifts all the way round the inside of one foot and the outer side of the other, through your toes, back down the other side and around your heels. Let your upper body go with the movement. Don't try to lean backwards or forwards if you feel unbalanced, just take it slowly and make small circles. Repeat in the opposite direction.

Knee Bobbing

Place the heels of your hands on top of the corresponding knee. Bend the knees as far as is comfortable keeping knee caps aligned with your toes and not passing the tips. Rise up to a standing position with legs straight and repeat.

Knee Circles

Place the heels of your hands on your knees as in the previous exercise, squat down slightly and move your legs down and round in a circle, rolling around the outsides of your feet. Repeat on other side.

This exercise is very popular in tai chi classes and opinion is split between those who feel it hurts or helps their knees. The former category may be moving too far forward, allowing their knees to reach beyond the toe tips. In any event, given that the knee moves primarily like a hinge and has limited ability to circle, the exercise is probably more useful for the ankles.

See **Notes On Knees** *below.*

If in doubt – don't do it.

Ankle Circles

Raise one leg so you are standing on the tips of your toes; the other foot is flat on the ground. Move the raised part of your foot in horizontal circles, keeping the knee facing forward. Repeat in the opposite direction.

Knee Bobbing   *Ankle Circles*   *Whole Body*

Swinging (Arms, Knees & Hips)

Stand on one leg and swing the other back and forth from the knee, whilst both arms swing at the same tempo. Do this about eighteen times each side. You should start to feel an elasticity behind your knees which aids the movement.

Now hold your knee straight so that the movement comes from the hips, continuing to swing your arms. Repeat eighteen times each side.

If you have trouble balancing for this movement, you can support yourself by placing a hand on something solid, although your arm movement will be restricted to one side if you do this. You can also try swinging both knees together by sitting on a surface of adequate height for your legs to dangle such as a desk or kitchen counter.

Whole Body

Move from side to side, lifting each leg up and across your body with knee bent, then straightening it slightly to kick lightly. The movement should come from your hips. At the same time, swing the corresponding arm up and across your chest, the impetus coming from the bottom of your shoulder blades. If you are sufficiently relaxed you should be able to move lightly and smoothly from foot to foot.

Some Notes On Knees

The knee is one of the largest and most complex joints in the body. However, it doesn't like being turned or placed under too much stress and is therefore at risk in any sporting activity.

I know many martial artists with immobile knees who have taken up tai chi because their previous sport has become too painful. Hyper-extension of the knees is a common injury in kicking sports and there are a range of other potential problems. Its position between the hip and ankle makes it vulnerable to injury resulting from the misplacement of either of these joints.

In theory tai chi is beneficial for knees, but there are potential problems here too, and you need to be aware of the following in particular:

Don't extend the knee beyond your toes

This is a common fault in forward and horse stances where leg strength is insufficient to support a low position, leading us to lean too far forward to try to maintain the stance.

Don't allow knee to sag inwards

This presents an even greater risk of injury as your twisted knee can end up supporting all your weight, damaging the joint and supporting tissue. This fault can occur in most stances, affecting forward or rear leg, and often goes unnoticed by student and teacher.

If your hips are properly open, your knees can't move inwards. Try taking a stance and tilting the pelvis forward. Your knees should automatically open outwards. If your hips aren't yet flexible enough, be aware of the danger and don't try to make your stances too long or low until your body is able to cope. Take any pain in your knees seriously.

CHAPTER 7 - Stretching

Stretching helps to prepare the mind and body for tai chi and tui shou practice. It is time consuming, there's no getting away from that fact. Like all exercise, it's easy to talk yourself out of doing it, especially when you are keen to get on with the tai chi itself. However, it's worth it. The benefits of stretching for life in general are now well documented and I've noted some of them below, together with others specific to tai chi.

Benefits of Stretching

- Reduce muscle tension
- Increase body comfort
- Increase energy levels
- Increase blood circulation
- Aid relaxation
- Relieve stress
- Increase power
- Lengthen muscle fibres
- Improve range of motion
- Move more naturally
- Improve posture
- Improve control of muscles
- Develop body awareness

- Increase balance and coordination
- Reduce susceptibility to injury
- Reduce fatigue
- Reduce post exercise soreness
- Remove lactic acid

Benefits For Tai Chi

These specific stretching exercises will enable you to get down lower, balance better and perform beautifully, movements such as Snake Creeps Down.

Stretching can diminish the reflexes which cause us to flinch or tighten our muscles when touched. This is particularly useful in partner practice.

As well as all this, it can improve the passage of qi through your body, as your joints open up and your body starts to become "Song" (the relaxed state to which tai chi practitioners should aspire).

Static Stretches

All the stretches in this book are static stretches, which means that they are performed from a stationary position. The body is moved slowly into a position where a muscle (or group of muscles) is placed under tension. The position is held for a minimum amount of time so that the muscles can relax and lengthen.

How to Stretch

- ◆ Warm-up before stretching for a few minutes, for example with a short walk or marching on the spot
- ◆ Make sure your position is stable, especially in the exercises where you stand on one leg; you may need something to hold on to
- ◆ Move gently into the stretch whilst exhaling
- ◆ Pay attention to your posture
- ◆ Keep your shoulders down and your chin tucked in
- ◆ Breath freely and evenly as you hold the stretch
- ◆ For best results perform each stretch twice, the first time for twenty seconds, and the second for a minute
- ◆ If you only stretch once, hold for a minute
- ◆ Stretch enough to feel tension, but not pain

Letting Go

When I started doing these exercises I didn't breath properly, and failed to understand that I needed to let go of my muscles to allow them to stretch. I stayed rigidly in position for a minute, with muscles contracted. Hence it took me a long time to start to feel the benefits. My mind was actually fighting my body and refusing to allow my muscles to stretch. Once I realised this and learned to let go my muscles began to respond and my body started changing rapidly.

The Stretch Reflex

If you attempt to over stretch, your body has a built in safety cut off switch, the *myotatic* or *stretch reflex*. This stops you damaging yourself by preventing the muscles from being over-stretched. Hence, you'll be wasting your time if you try to do too much.

Focus on Stretching

Try to look at the time spent stretching as a meditation and preparation for your tai chi practice. Slowly counting as you breathe helps you to focus and quieten your mind, as well as aiding the stretching process.

Balanced Stretching

Don't forget to stretch antagonistic muscle groups. Each muscle has an opposing one and it is vital to train them both to ensure your body is balanced and one group does not gain in flexibility whilst the other tightens.

Hold that Stretch

Don't be tempted to shorten the time spent holding the stretches. It takes the muscle about twenty seconds to relax, and it is after this point that it starts to lengthen.

It's essential to stretch for enough time, and also to do it regularly if you want to keep the benefits. If you stop it is likely that your muscles will quickly return to their previous level of flexibility.

Check your Progress

Before starting the routine, you may want to assess your flexibility so you can measure the results. You can purchase an inexpensive protractor-like device specifically for this purpose online. Alternatively, you can just measure the position reached, although the readings won't be as accurate.

Flexibility Assessment

Shoulders

Do the **Meeting Hands Stretch** (see below) and record the distance between your hands or the amount of overlap.

Hamstrings

Lie down on your back with arms by your sides. Raise one leg up keeping it straight and the other flat on the floor. Measure the angle of your hip at the furthest point. Repeat with your other leg.

Back, Hips & Hamstrings

Sit on the floor with legs straight and feet flat against a small box or similar item. Bend forward towards your toes as far as you can. Measure the distance of your reach in relation to the box.

Ankles

Do the **Toes Up Stretch** (see below) far enough away from your immoveable object that your hip is just touching it. Measure the height your toes reach.

The Stretches

LOWER LEGS

Toes Up Stretch

Using a pole, tree or other vertical solid object, bring one foot as close as possible with toes facing upwards and your other foot flat on the ground. Grasp the pole to bring yourself closer. Hold.

Area worked – ankle, calf, Achilles

Toe Drop Stretch

Find a curb or other drop longer than your foot. Rest the middle of the heel on the edge and reach downwards.

Area worked – ankle, shin

Note

In many people the ankles are very stiff and inflexible. This, even more than stiff hips or knees, may be the reason they are unable to descend into low postures.

Toes Up Stretch 1   *Toes Up Stretch 2*   *Toe Drop Stretch*

LEGS & HIPS

Inwards Leg Up Stretch

Place one leg out straight on a horizontal bar or other surface approx mid-thigh height. Lean forward to take hold of your toes keeping your knee in line and turn your foot inwards whilst turning the hip of your standing leg inwards at the same time. The standing foot points straight ahead.

Repeat with other leg. Increase to approx chest height and repeat. Increase again if possible. You are looking to do a progressive stretch at three heights of regular intervals. In time you may be able to reach your own height or even beyond, depending on your determination and body's limits.

Outwards Leg Up Stretch

Follow the instructions for the inward Leg Up Stretch, but turn the raised foot to the outside and turn your standing foot out the other way, at 90 degrees to the bar or as much as your hips allow.

Area worked – hamstrings

Open Leg Up Stretch

As per the previous stretch, but this time let your raised foot reach forward. The standing leg is again turned outwards. Repeat with progressive heights as before.

Area worked - hamstrings, hips

Inwards Leg Up Stretch　　*Outwards Leg Up Stretch*　　*Open Leg Up Stretch*

Bent Over Hamstring Stretch

Stand with feet shoulder width apart, legs straight. Bend forward from the waist allowing your head and arms to hang down.

Bent Over Hamstring Stretch (variation)

This time stand with your legs straight, feet together. Bend forward from the waist and wrap your arms around your legs, pulling your upper body inwards. This gives you more of a stretch but is considerably more difficult.

Area worked – hamstrings, knees

Maxi Stretch

Place one foot on the upper level of a horizontal surface which has bars at hip height and below. Your knee is bent and other leg is straight out behind with foot pointing forward. Press forward with your hips, bringing your body towards the bar and place your hands on the lower level. Think of trying to get your shoulders all the way forward.

Area worked – hip flexors, quads, calves, hamstrings, glutes, lower back

100

*Bent Over Hamstrings
Stretch*   *Bent Over Hamstrings
(variation)*   *Maxi Stretch*

Adductor Stretch

Squat down in front of a park bench or similar object. One leg is extended straight out to the side with foot pointing upwards and the other is bent at the knee with foot flat on the ground. Make sure your foot and knee are in alignment. Lean forward and grasp the bench, at the same time arching your spine downwards.

If your ankle is not flexible enough to allow your foot to stay flat to begin with, you can prop up your heel with a wedge or stone.

Area worked – hip adductors, lower back, hamstrings, glutes, calves

Adductor Stretch 1   *Adductor Stretch 2*

Snake Creeping Stretch

Squat down with one leg bent and the other out at 90 degrees, feet flat on the ground. Use a post or other solid object (such as a heavy chair or bed) to push the heel of your straight leg out and pull the toes inwards towards your centre. Make sure there is no pressure on your knee by turning the hip so that your leg turns slightly inwards. Again, if you lack flexibility you can slide a small object under your heel.

Area worked - more for mobility than flexibility, this exercise helps you gain the ability to perform one of the most challenging tai chi movements. It stretches the ankle, but as you will not feel the muscle stretching, it is important to hold for at least a minute.

Snake Creeping Stretch   *Snake Creeping : foot position*

Note

For the first year practising the above two stretches, I used progressively smaller stones until I was finally able to discard them altogether!

Hip Mobility Stretch (external rotator)

Bend your leg against the edge of a horizontal surface at approx hip height with foot facing outwards. Your other leg is straight with the foot at right angles. Face the surface and press your hips forward and away.

Area worked – hips, glutes

Bent Leg Hip Stretch (internal rotator)

Rest your bent leg on the edge of a horizontal surface at approx hip height with foot pointing into your centre. With your other leg straight and foot pointing ahead, grasp the surface and press your hips forward.

These two stretches are important for any forward movement in tai chi. Your hips will open more easily enabling you to bring your legs up, out and forward in a circular motion and back to centre with a similar smooth movement.

Quad Stretch

Use a vertical object for support and stand against it with one leg bent behind you, keeping the knee pointing straight down. Drop your hips and push forward. Your standing leg is slightly bent at the knee. It is important to keep your pelvis forward so you do not strain your back.

Area worked – hip flexors, psoas, quads

| Bent Leg Hip Stretch | Hip Mobility Stretch | Quad Stretch |

THE UPPER BODY

Reaching Side Stretch

Stand with feet shoulder width apart, hips and knees relaxed. Raise one arm and bend over to the opposite side with the other hand reaching down your leg. Don't bend forward. Repeat on other side.

Reaching Side Stretch (variation)

Hold on to a horizontal surface with the hand which is reaching over your head, and pull back towards the stretching side. Put your other arm across your waist to prevent you from leaning inwards. Repeat on the other side. This gives a stronger stretch.

Area worked – oblique abdominals, lower back

Rotation Stretch

Stand with feet shoulder width apart in front of a tree or post. Soften your knees and tuck your pelvis in. Turn your waist and upper body to the side, placing the arm furthest away against the post to enable you to turn further. Keep knees facing forward.

Area worked – oblique abdominals and lower back

Reaching Side Stretch   *Reaching Side Stretch*   *Rotation Stretch*
                                 (variation)

Outer Forearm Stretch

Hold your arm straight out in front of you at shoulder height with your palm facing the ground. Grip your hand with the other one. Now push the hand straight back towards your body, keeping your arm extended. Repeat on other side.

Inner Forearm Stretch

Hold your arm straight out with palm facing up. Now grip your hand with the other one and pull back towards your body while your arm remains extended.

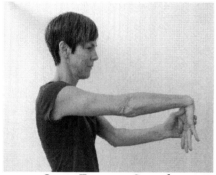 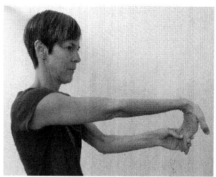

Outer Forearm Stretch   *Inner Forearm Stretch*

THE SHOULDERS

Arms Up Shoulder Stretch

Stand with feet shoulder width apart. Interlace fingers above your head with palms facing up. Push upwards using your back and shoulder blades.

Area worked – shoulders, upper back, arms, hands, fingers and wrists

Arms Forward Shoulder Stretch

Stand with feet shoulder width apart. Interlace fingers in front of you and press palms forward.

Area worked – shoulders, upper back, arms, hands, fingers and wrists

Arms Behind Back Stretch

Interlace your fingers behind your back and with your arms straight pull upwards as far as you can. You can either stay in an upright position or bend forward from the hips if you prefer.

Area worked – shoulders, pectorals

 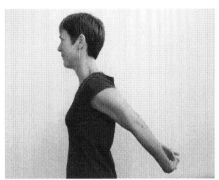

Arms Forward Shoulder Stretch   *Arms Behind Back Stretch*

Meeting Hands Stretch

Raise one arm straight up and bend elbow, reaching down to your shoulder blade. With the elbow of your other arm pointing towards the floor, reach up with palm facing out to grasp the fingers of your other hand.

If your hands are unable to meet at first, take a towel in the first hand and hold it with the other. In time you will be able to bring your hands closer together and eventually discard the towel.

Area worked – shoulders, shoulder blades, upper arms

  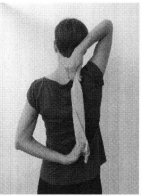

Arms Up Shoulder
Stretch

Meeting Hands
Stretch

Meeting Hands
(variation)

THE BACK

Back Arch Stretch

Kneel with palms directly below your armpits and knees below the hip crease. Put a towel under your ankles if they are stiff. Tuck your chin in. Press your hands and knees into the ground, lift your buttocks and push your spine up towards the ceiling, moving your hips slightly back so that the stretch targets your lower back.

Spine Stretch

Kneel down on all fours. Pull your bottom back towards your heels, whilst stretching your arms ahead of you. If this is uncomfortable at first, try placing a folded towel between buttocks and legs. Move slowly back and forward a few times to extend your range before you hold the extended position.

Area worked – these exercises are very important for developing sensitivity and flexibility within the spine. This is an area which is stiff in many people and has lost the natural articulation with which we are born. The exercises free up the pelvis and relax the back so that movements are more natural and the stance is strong and correctly aligned.

Back Arch Stretch

Spine Stretch

安乐

CHAPTER 8 – Mobility

The ability to move freely and easily

In tai chi, we are looking for our body to move easily and comfortably, with as great a range as we can achieve. Modern life, especially in the West, demands that from around the age of five years, we learn to stifle our natural instincts.

At school we have to carry sacks of heavy books on our backs then sit still for hours. At home, we sit down again, this time in front of the TV or computer, which seem to have replaced more active games for the majority of children. By the time we reach adolescence, many of us are in such a state of tension that our jaws, buttocks, hips, stomachs and shoulders are constantly clenched, even while we sleep.

The mobility exercises in this book are designed to help recapture the range of movement most of us have lost. How many adults can squat down on their heels? Not many in the West, but in Asia it's a daily occurrence which people in their eighties can manage with ease.

If you don't use a facility, you run the risk of losing it, but with time and effort it can be regained. Like riding a bike...

The Exercises

Hip Rotations

Place one leg up on a horizontal surface at approximately waist height. Rotate the heel of your standing leg away from your body and at the same time rotate the hip of the raised leg in the same direction. Make sure you breathe out with your stomach and hips tucked in as you make the movement, otherwise you will block your hips from rotating.

Return to the starting position, again on an out breath. If this is easy, try a greater height. Make sure you have something to hold on to when doing this exercise. Repeat nine times each side.

Hip Rotations 1

Hip Rotations 2

Spine Circles

Imagine you have a ball inside your abdomen. Stand with feet a little more than shoulder width apart and arms relaxed. Start with the ball at the location of your dantian, about two fingers' width below and three fingers' width behind your belly button. Move your whole body with the ball, starting in a slight squat, and rising to your full height when the ball reaches its highest point.

Now roll the ball up the front of your stomach across the top of your chest and down your back. Push it right up against the wall of your stomach and your spine. Repeat eighteen times, then reverse the direction. Again starting at the dantian, push the ball up your spine across and down your front, moving your body simultaneously.

The movement relaxes your internal organs and opens your body so that qi can circulate smoothly. It also works the muscles of your abdomen, which in many people are under-used. In qi gong there are similar exercises which aim to propel qi around the body.

3 Axis Circles

This series of exercises involves making circular motions with the hips, waist, ribs, chest and shoulders successively. Each part is rolled forward then backwards in three different dimensions. Start with feet shoulder width apart, hips and knees relaxed.

Imagine that your hip turns around an axle, like a wheel. Hold your index-finger against the top of your hip bone, facing straight inwards. This is the axis around which you move your hip in circles, first one way and then the other. The second axis is on the side of the hip bone, finger facing towards your centre. The third points straight down. One side rotates along with the hip, the other side stays as still as possible.

Repeat each of the six actions nine times in each direction for each hip, and then for the other areas in turn.

It is likely that your body will be quite stiff to start with. The increased mobility will help you perform tai chi movements correctly. It is also very useful in tui shou, giving you the ability to move an individual body part in response to your partner's push.

Expansion Circles

Take a forward stance with feet shoulder width apart but a little longer than usual, which will increase your stability. Extend the arm on the side of your forward foot ahead of you as far as possible, pointing your index finger ahead as far as your body will allow (probably further than you think). Then draw a big circle in the air, moving your body and keeping your arm extended. The circle comes up above your head then back behind you and along the ground before returning to the start. Keep your eyes fixed on your pointing finger at all times.

Repeat the circle nine times, then draw a circle which starts behind you, rises over your head and comes down in front of you. Pivot on heels and toes to allow the movement. Now do the circles with the opposite arm before changing legs and repeating each of the four parts (forward and backwards with arm on same and opposing side as forward leg).

You can also do the circles across the front of your body and out to the sides. Again, reach out as far as you can and repeat with both arms on each side.

This exercise really gives you a feel for your body's possibilities. You may fall over, and that's actually a good thing, because it means that you're truly beginning to understand your limits.

Expansion Circles 1   *Expansion Circles 2*   *Expansion Circles 3*

Note

The human body is naturally lazy and often does the minimum it can get away with. One could contend that it does not expend unnecessary energy. The problem with this argument is that when you do want greater mobility, you find that your body has lost its original range and is actually becoming more and more restricted.

Plate Balancing

Start with feet a little more than shoulder width apart and hands out in front of you, palms upwards. Start with one plate. Move the plate up, down and around you by keeping your palm face up and moving your arm and whole body. In order to get the plate above your head, you will need to relax the hips forward and move underneath your arm.

Plate Balancing 1

Plate Balancing 2

Plate Balancing 3   *Plate Balancing 4*

Try the other plate, and two plates at once. You can circle your arms in the same or opposite directions. Do this exercise for about a minute, or more if you're enjoying it. You can practice with real plates, though plastic or imaginary ones are probably best until you've got a good grasp of the technique. Eventually, it can make a great party trick when serving the dinner.

CHAPTER 9 - Breathing & Relaxation

Breathing correctly is important in tai chi, so it is necessary to understand a little about the mechanics. "To be more relaxed" is frequently cited as a reason for taking up tai chi, but at first it can seem as if all it's doing is highlighting how chronically tense you are.

This is the first step on the road to relaxation and a more comfortable life, so don't look on it as a negative. In order to heal ourselves we need to know what our problems are.

We are equipped to breathe in a variety of different ways, and should be able to adapt to individual situations. The best way to breathe is to use the nose, which filters, humidifies and adjusts the temperature of air before it enters your body.

You should also be using your diaphragm to breathe. The diaphragm is a dome-shaped layer of muscle which lies horizontally around the bottom of your ribs and is attached to your lungs. Your heart and lungs are situated above it, and your stomach, intestines and liver below. When you breathe in, it should move downward, stretching the lungs at the same time. The resultant space in the lungs is filled with the air inhaled, and the ribs and chest also expand. The diaphragm then relaxes and rises up again, pushing the air out.

This type of breathing is known variously as belly, abdominal, diaphragmatic, post-birth and Buddhist breathing. It is generally considered best for tai chi, although it is not the traditional way. (See the note below on reverse breathing.)

Another form of breathing, commonly referred to as "complete breathing", engages the lungs fully and is widely used in yoga. This is also a very healthy way to breathe, but is not used in tai chi. The abdomen is the home of your lower dantian, and thus the focus for tai chi breathing.

Breathing Habits

In the West many people have poor breathing habits, and this affects both their health and posture. Common issues include *mouth breathing, over breathing, front ribcage breathing, upper chest breathing and reverse breathing.*

♦ **Mouth breathing**

Breathing through the mouth causes increased susceptibility to illness and nasal congestion, as well as being a common characteristic of snorers. Although we *can* breathe through the mouth, it does not act as a filter in the way that the nose does and is therefore seldom a good option in normal activity.

♦ **Over breathing**

This is another word for hyperventilation, the acute version of which you may have experienced in a stressful situation. Inhaling too much air results in an imbalance of oxygen and carbon dioxide, which makes you feel breathless or dizzy. Thus you again inhale too much air and the situation persists. A surprising number of people suffer from chronic hyperventilation, often unknowingly. The symptoms are various and include light headedness, chest pains, cold extremities, digestive problems, premature ageing, insomnia and depression.

♦ **Front ribcage and upper chest breathing**

Both are examples of shallow breathing, where air enters only the upper part of the lungs and the diaphragm is raised, so that it cannot expand. Shallow breathing is very inefficient, as it's not possible to get much air into the lungs. As the diaphragm does not descend, there is no resultant stretching of the lungs. It also precludes the beneficial massaging action of the diaphragm against the internal organs, which happens in abdominal breathing.

All the above ways of breathing evolved as ways to respond to emergency situations and each causes or results from tension within the body. Upper abdominal tension blocks the diaphragm from descending and the chest from lifting. Tension in the spine prevents the ribs from expanding, which restricts breathing. Tension due to lack of movement in the diaphragm causes neck problems (the scalenes act as accessory muscles of inhalation as well as aiding with neck movement and if they are employed inappropriately will be subject to unnecessary wear).

Breathe & Relax

In tai chi, we are looking to relax both physically and mentally. Breathing correctly helps with this in a number of ways. Using the diaphragm generates pressure in the abdomen which helps to stabilise the trunk. Using the back muscles to inhale extends the spine; if the spine is stiff the breathing muscles work harder without gain. Nose breathing slows the process down which means you breathe in a more leisurely fashion. It has the opposite effect of the unhelpful ways mentioned above, actually acting to slow your heart rate and relax your muscles.

So the goal is to breathe through the nose and into the abdomen. All the time, not just when doing tai chi. The exercises below should be done daily if possible. It takes a long time for the body to learn new habits but you'll probably notice improvements in your general health pretty quickly and want to persevere.

Once you are able to bring your new breathing skills and more relaxed body into your tai chi, you can start trying to think about using the breath in your form. Each gesture should accord with a breath: inhalations for yin or passive movements, and exhalations for yang or assertive movements. I know quite a few teachers are reluctant to cover breathing in their tai chi lessons. The idea is that it is confusing for beginners who already have so much else to think about when practising tai chi. However, if you do not breath correctly, you stand little chance of being able to relax sufficiently to do tai chi. My philosophy, therefore, is to ensure students have good breathing habits right from the start, although it may be a long time before it is appropriate to think about synchronising the breath with the movements in your form.

A Note About Reverse Breathing

Reverse breathing is the action of pulling your abdomen in on the inhalation and pushing it out on the exhalation. In theory it is the correct way to breathe in tai chi as pushing out the abdomen adds power to the gestures. Reverse breathing is usually a response to shock and as a habit is common in people who have experienced some kind of trauma. It doesn't calm your body. In fact, it has the *reverse* effect.

This fits if you are doing tai chi as if it were a fighting art and trying to bring meaning into the martial applications of the movements. For most people, though, especially in the first years of practising, the calming abdominal breathing method is the more appropriate.

The Exercises

Belly Breathing

Standing with feet shoulder width apart and arms by your sides, relax and breathe deeply into your abdomen, letting your belly inflate as you inhale and retract as you exhale. The weight of your stomach moving should propel your body gently forward and back on your feet as you breathe. Humans are largely made of water and thus it is natural that we move slightly all the time. Do this exercise for about two minutes or until you feel relaxed.

Abdominal Workout

Lie down on your back with your head supported and your legs straight out or bent at the knees with feet flat on the floor. Keep your mouth closed throughout. Take a deep breath in whilst pushing your lower abdomen out as far as you can. Try to inflate the whole area, like a balloon. When you have inhaled as much as you can, let the air out whilst sucking your stomach right in as far as possible. Imagine you are trying to get your belly button to touch your back.

You may find it helpful to put your hands on your belly to feel the movement. You can also check you are exhaling at the right moment by putting a hand up to your face to feel the out breath. Keep breathing like this for ten minutes, or more if you feel able.

This exercise is for people with tense stomachs. It relaxes the abdominal muscles and massages the internal organs. It allows you to start the process of using your diaphragm correctly, which you should aim to do all the time. If you do the exercise before going to sleep, you should find your rest is enhanced. Do this exercise as often as possible.

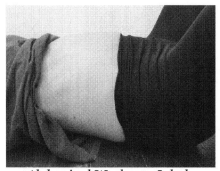

Abdominal Workout - Inhale   *Abdominal Workout - Exhale*

The Reviver

Lie down on your back, on the floor or an exercise mat, with your legs comfortably bent a little wider than your hips, feet flat on the floor. Put two or three paperback books under your head, high enough so that your neck is level with your spine. You are looking to have your chin tucked in and your back touching the floor along its whole length. Let your body relax into the floor, and stay in position for at least fifteen minutes.

This exercise is based on the F M Alexander Technique Semi-Supine Position and is a great way to put your spine back into alignment, after it has been deformed by a day sitting in chairs, driving, using computers and so on. The technique is more complicated than my version, and you are encouraged to stay alert to your bodily sensations. You can do this, but you can also use it as a time to relax body and mind.

I find if I'm tired but have more things to do it refreshes me far more than a caffeine fix. A friend who suffers from chronic fatigue syndrome has switched from sleeping for two hours in the afternoons to doing the exercise for just fifteen or twenty minutes, and finds it has the same or more benefit.

The Reviver

Back Breathing

Back Breathing

Kneel on the floor with your feet together and knees spread apart as far as is comfortable. Place your forehead on the floor with arms in a relaxed position either side of your head. Let go of your head and body, sinking into the floor. As you breathe, fill your whole torso, feeling your ribs move outwards and backwards as they expand with each incoming breath.

Progressive Muscle Relaxation

Lie on your back, on the floor or an exercise mat, with your head supported, legs flat out along the floor with feet apart, and arms comfortably along your sides. Start by breathing in your abdomen, slowly and deeply. Repeat the word "relax" to yourself several times. Next you will tense and then relax each major muscle group in turn. Breathe in as you contract and out as you let go. Tense for about five seconds each time, then relax for fifteen or so afterwards.

Hands/arms - make your hands into fists. Tense them as hard as you can. Then let go, let your hands flop and your arms relax into the floor.

Neck/shoulders – pull your shoulders up towards your ears, as high as you can. Release and feel the tension drain out.

Face/jaw – screw up your eyes, clench your jaw and bite your teeth together. As you relax, feel your face smoothing out and leave your jaw just closed with teeth parted. Let your head sink into the pillow.

Legs/feet – brace your legs against the floor whilst pulling your toes towards your head. Then slacken the tension and let them flop.

Whole body – now try to be aware of your whole body and notice any remaining areas of tension. Repeat the exercise for any part where you feel it's necessary. Carry on breathing slowly and deeply. Stay in place for a little while, enjoying the feeling that your whole body and also your mind have unwound a little.

Progressive Muscle Relaxation has been around since the 1930s. It was pioneered by Edward Jacobson as a means of identifying and tackling tension and variants are now widely used, especially for insomnia. If it's not a good time to fall asleep, you may want to set an alarm clock when you do this exercise!

CHAPTER 10 – Swimming

Okay, so what's a chapter entitled "Swimming" doing in a book of exercises related to tai chi?

I appreciate that for many people swimming is not as easy or enjoyable as doing tai chi. There's travel to the pool, unpleasant changing rooms, worry over hygiene, water not sufficiently heated or over-chlorinated, damage to hair, goggle marks and embarrassment about body shape, to name but a few common excuses.

But if you can get over them, swimming is in itself a wonderful relaxing activity. In addition, regular swimming can aid tai chi progress in a number of ways.

I have found a remarkable symmetry between the two activities and as I became more aware of individual parts of my body in my tai chi practice, so I was able to apply what I had learned to swimming and feed my development in the pool back into the tai chi.

Breathing

Getting the breathing right when you're swimming is very important. In order to obtain the health benefits you have to put your face in the water. Head out of water breast-strokers are doing terrible damage to their spines. Better to not swim at all than swim like this. The illustration below shows how the vertebrae are compressed in this practice.

If you find it difficult to put your face in the water, first get a pair of goggles, then practice just putting your face in whilst standing in shallow water, or at home in the bathroom. After this, you can start breast stroke with face in every few breaths and eventually progress to doing all the strokes without difficulty. For me, this took just a couple of months swimming for half an hour twice a week.

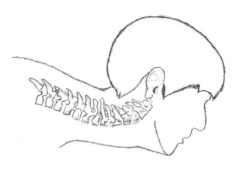

Correct breathing in swimming can improve your stamina and position in the water. The technique is not the same as for tai chi, though, being one of the few activities where it's a good idea to breathe with your mouth. In all strokes, the inhalation should be quite short, just before you put your head in the water. Your exhalation should be twice as long as your inhalation, a long smooth out-breath blowing bubbles into the water.

Our upper bodies are more buoyant than the lower half, which can cause legs and hips to lie too low, preventing us skimming lightly across the water. Limiting the amount of air in your chest will reduce this effect, as will allowing your head to sink naturally. A subconscious fear of drowning often prevents us from relaxing in the water, and the tension inhibits our ability to move freely.

Elegant High Kicking

Once you're swimming with confidence, you can start experimenting with all kinds of sensations connected with tai chi. I'd recommend trying the following exercises one session at a time to start with, until you get a real feeling for your body in the water.

No Swimming Exercises

Tai Chi Form

Tai chi teachers often suggest practising as if you were in water. Water provides resistance, so that movements have to be done slowly and precisely. It is interesting to experiment with actual as well as imaginary water. For this you need chest high water of a comfortable temperature.

Try to do your form. It's very hard, but the experience gives you valuable insight into the circular movements of tai chi – in water you cannot move in a straight line. It's also a good exercise in concentration, as you have to move very slowly and accurately if you don't want to float away.

Push Hands

You can also try practising push hands (tui shou) in the sea, pitting yourself against the waves as if they were your partner.

Ankle Flexing

Rigid ankles are very common in adults and a real impediment to swimming, not to mention doing tai chi. Sit on the side of the pool and flex your ankles back and forth and in circles in the water.

Leg Lifts

If you find yourself unable to kick higher than your phantom opponent's shins, your instructor will probably tell you that it's fine, as lower leg kicks can be more effective and you yourself are less vulnerable in your imaginary combat if your leg is not raised too high. This is perfectly true, but somewhat contra the spirit of tai chi, which looks to open joints and release taut muscles. Also, as I pointed out in the section on mobility, if you don't utilise your range of movement, you'll lose it. Thirdly, as with low snakes, high kicks look graceful and elegant.

Your limited range may be the result of a lack of strength in the abdominal area – your "corset" muscles, which prevents you from staying upright on one leg. It could also be related to supporting leg strength or that of the thigh in the leg which is raised. Whatever the reason, you can practise static leg lifts, straight out in front for heel kicks and slightly to the side for toe kicks. Hold on to something for stability and keep the leg extended for as long as possible. This exercise, rather unpleasant on dry land, becomes enjoyable and much easier when performed in water.

In chest deep water, touching the side of the pool with the arm on the same side as your supporting leg, bring your other leg up in front of you as high as you can, and keep it there for up to one minute. Repeat at an angle of 45 degrees, and then again on the other side.

Swimming Exercises

Dantian Rolling - front and back crawl

Initiate movement from your centre. Each stroke of your arm comes from the dantian – just like in tai chi. The body moves as one unit, rather than separate parts all doing their own thing.

Elasticity - front and back crawl

Reach out from your torso, rather than just moving your arms. This makes swimming much less tiring. The strokes have a voluntary and involuntary phase – feel the elasticity in your body as your arm reaches out and then springs back.

Use More Muscles - back stroke

The back muscles are often underused, and working them can help with the problem of round shoulders. Make sure you swim on your back as often as on your front, and consciously initiate the movement of your arms from the middle of your back. Lift the small of your back to prevent your legs sinking and causing drag.

Open the Hips - breast stroke

The open leg movements are great for releasing tight hip muscles.

Immobility in Movement - breast stroke and butterfly

Extend your arms then bring your body forward to meet them, rather than pulling the arms back. This mirrors the movement of a well executed tai chi form, where the arms follow the body.

Mobility in Movement - all strokes

Just like in the 3 axis circle exercises, you can use your hips and shoulders in a circular motion to progress through the water. Concentrate on moving the joints rather than your arms and legs, which should just follow along naturally.

Just Swimming

In common with walking and jogging, swimming belongs to the group of exercises which are beneficial to the body because they circulate lactic acid. More strenuous activities like running and working out in the gym can result in muscle soreness, cramp and fatigue. A session in the pool the day after can relieve or even prevent these symptoms.

What about tai chi, you ask? Well, tai chi is actually a little too slow to have this effect. It is necessary for the heart and breathing to speed up a bit when you're exercising for lactic acid circulation to occur.

CHAPTER 11 – Every Day Life

When you begin practising tai chi, it is likely that you will soon begin to have a heightened awareness of your body at all times. For me, this meant an awareness of uneconomical action resulting in wasted energy and undue physical strain. To change postural habits takes a long time. After all, most people have probably spent decades doing repetitive tasks in the same way.

Try to be aware of tension in normal life by stopping and noticing if you have any muscles clenched or are moving awkwardly. For example, clenching your jaw or gripping things with your hands. When I started doing this I was immediately aware of my stomach muscles tightening up in response to just about any physical activity as well as emotional stimuli and was even waking up in the mornings with a sore abdomen. The more aware of your body you become the more you will notice these things and your search for greater comfort may initially be a very uncomfortable experience.

Tight clothes are restrictive as are many shoes and even belts and bras. Often people are quite unaware of their discomfort and it is only as their bodies start to relax that they can address it, rather than waiting for old age to set in and the whole structure to seize up.

When you start to examine how you do things, it is likely that you will find that you grip items too tightly, bend and reach awkwardly, hold your breath, stick your chin out, arch your back or any number of other actions designed to cause internal stress, both physical and mental.

By slowing down and examining how you move, you can start to address these issues and use your body more sympathetically. Good posture gives you more energy and confidence. Your body becomes more comfortable and less vulnerable to injury.

Of course, we can also progress in tai chi more quickly if we start using our bodies more effectively during the many hours when we're unable to practise. Better posture, breathing and a more relaxed body with parts that move in collaboration are all important factors in well-executed tai chi. Below I have examined some common areas where using tai chi principles can enrich our lives, as well as our tai chi.

As your sensitivity improves, you will develop a progressively greater awareness of when you are not using your body correctly and can continue to make adjustments to the way you carry out every day tasks.

Mindfulness

In all these exercises, in fact as much of the time as you can manage, try to put your whole consciousness into the action. This is what Buddhists call mindfulness. Concentrate fully on what you're doing. Note the sensations you feel and how your body is responding. This not only helps you find a better way to accomplish things, but also has the effect of calming your mind. These days it's considered desirable to be able to "multi-task" but doing several tasks and thinking about multiple subjects all at once is a recipe for doing nothing well and causing mental confusion.

When you are mindful you are living in the moment. Mindfulness allows us to review our actions and methods and adjust them as appropriate. If you can bring this tranquil mental state into your tai chi, you will make considerable progress.

Sinking

I'm going to start with a small exercise in imagination.

You've being doing tai chi for a while now, and have finally booked that trip to China, two weeks travelling around by train, bus and aeroplane visiting the Chen Village, Wudang Mountains, Great Wall, Yellow River and so on.

You're leaving the Bureau de Change with an envelope full of Chinese Yuan when a villain bumps into you and you drop it on the ground. Can you retrieve the envelope before he picks it up and runs off?

You're not very good at bending down, perhaps due to wearing high heeled shoes a lot. In class, you find it hard to reach below mid calf.

Normally you stoop, bending forward from the waist, in order to pick things up, but at the moment you've got a bit of a bad back and you don't want to aggravate it when you'll soon be spending fifteen hours on a plane...If you move quickly perhaps you can beat the thief, but you run the risk of acute or chronic injury to your back, putting that China trip in jeopardy.

Fortunately, help is at hand in the form of your friend who's been doing tai chi for some years, has followed all the exercises in this book and is able to drop nimbly to the ground, whisking the envelope out of harm's way. But as she hands it to you, she says "You do know we'll have to use squat toilets in China, don't you?"

Typical Chinese Toilet

Stooping or bending from the waist puts strain on your lower back. There is lots of advice on how to bend down and lift things, which will go something like this:

The item to be lifted should not be too heavy. Position yourself directly in front of and close to it, with legs shoulder width apart. Relax the hips, breathe out and bend both hips and knees to assume a squatting position, keeping your spine straight. Bring the item close to you, holding it lightly but firmly. To lift, breathe out again to engage your core muscles. Keep the load close to you, your back straight, and never twist or turn your body. Keep your feet firmly on the ground pressing your weight down as you lift using the muscles of your legs.

This is great advice, but there's a problem with it. Most people are unable to keep their back straight and feet flat, and will instead stick their bottom out, so that the vertebrae are pushed out of alignment. In order to drop to the ground and rise up again with a straight back, you need a flexibility not usually found in the West.

The Snake Creeps Down posture, found in Yang and some other styles of tai chi, is one of the most challenging movements to perform well. It is necessary to sink down into a squatting position with your weight on one leg, then transfer the weight to the other leg and rise up into Golden Rooster Stands On One Leg.

If you are unable to do it in one fluid movement with your back straight, you are probably trying to sink down too low and should stay with a controlled high or medium position so that your spine is correctly positioned. This is illustrated below.

Snake Creeps Down

High position

Middle position

Low position

Incorrect position

The Exercises

Sinking

For this exercise you need a baton or broom handle. Hold it vertically behind your back with both arms and position yourself a few inches away from a wall. Your legs should be about one and a half times shoulder width apart, and your feet can face straight ahead or out to the sides (the latter makes the exercise easier). Descend with feet flat on the floor, letting your knees separate out to the sides. You will feel when you start to incline because the baton will begin touching the wall. Return to your lowest straight-backed position and stay there for a minute.

Do this exercise every day, and you will be able to get lower and lower. Your ultimate aim is eventually to discard the baton and descend right to the ground and up again with your back against the wall. Take it easy, though, being careful not to strain the knees by letting them bear your weight.

Placing a piece of wood or similar item under your heels may help you to descend much lower before you start to incline. The height of your prop can be lowered as your ankles gain flexibility, as with the Snake Creeping and Adductor stretches. Photos 1 & 2 show how much easier it is to sink with a straight back if the heels are raised. Photo 3 illustrates how the back may begin to curve if you try to keep the feet flat on the floor and facing straight ahead.

Sinking 1   *Sinking 2*   *Sinking 3 - incorrect*

Comment

Most people find this difficult due to a lack of flexibility in their ankles and strength in their thighs. Because we habitually use chairs we are not accustomed to bending beyond their level, and will collapse if we try to go further. Many emergency calls to fallen elderly people are as a result of their inability to rise again, rather than actual injury.

Lifestyle in the East, whilst in many ways poorer than that in the West, does not give rise to this issue. With people squatting to eat, socialise and use the toilet, the legs retain their ability to drop to ground level and get back up again without effort. If you watch very young children, you will see that they too have this skill, whereas if they tried to stick their bottoms out behind them they would immediately fall over. We lose this aptitude as a result of modern conveniences.

Tennis Ball Massage

This section includes several exercises which use a tennis ball, a cheap and effective aid to relaxation. I would also like to mention the tennis ball's similarity to the yin yang symbol. If you have time and a full marker pen, you can make your own yin yang tennis ball and contemplate yin yang theory and how the ball may resemble your own dantian.

Every day, spend a minute slowly rolling the tennis ball around under every part of your foot, including the sides, heel and toes, pressing as much weight on it as possible. Switch feet and repeat.

This will release tension in the fascia of your foot, which tracks right up your legs, through your pelvic floor, your internal organs and up to the crown of your head, as well as running out to your arms and hands.

The exercise therefore has the potential to stretch every part of your body. You can test this by bending down to touch your toes before and after massaging your feet. You should find you can stretch further the second time.

With an extra ball or two, you could also improve your coordination skills by practising juggling or massage any area of your body which feels like it needs it (place two balls in a sock for large or tricky areas).

144

Tension

Shoulder and neck tension are very common, and often caused by a lack of kinaesthetic awareness. People can't feel which muscles they are using to perform tasks and consequently employ too much or inappropriate effort. It's also common to go about tasks which we're not enjoying in a tense fashion, for example, gripping tools too hard when doing chores, holding our breath or turning and reaching awkwardly.

Around The House

For this exercise, spend a little time doing the housework using the following principles:

◆ Use all your fingers to hold a knife, cloth or other implement. The four and fifth fingers are commonly underused, and bringing them into tasks connects our hands with the shoulder blades and spine, lessening unnecessary activity in the upper shoulders.

- Don't grip tightly. Note how you hold on to anything from a door handle to a sponge. The chances are you're holding it too firmly and thus blocking the sensitive feeling available to you via the fingers, one of the most sensitive parts of the body. Increased sensitivity is yet another skill we search for in tai chi and it also makes doing tasks more pleasurable.

- Breathe. Notice if you're holding your breath. Slow down and breathe out when you expend effort, relaxing your pelvis at the same time.

- Pay attention to your posture at all times, especially standing at the sink or basin when you may well find yourself positioned awkwardly, stretching from too far away and with hips rigidly held forward. Relax your pelvis, adjust the distance and remember the points above.

Sex

Exercises designed to free up the body for tai chi, such as hip circles, can bring improvements to your sex life. Mobile hips and pelvis allow for a greater range of movement and access to a greater variety of positions. Nimble fingers increase sensitivity in foreplay.

For the serious student, it's also possible to regard sex as a warm up for tai chi, the positions stretching exercises and finger-play increasing mobility for hand gestures. The listening energy which is necessary for skilful push hands can be sharpened by sensitively caressing your partner.

An orgasm is said to enrich women's yin energy and exchange of bodily fluids to increase the qi flow in both partners. Some schools of thought do maintain, however, that ejaculation is exhausting for men and drains their Jing.

Finger Flex

Roll your thumb across each fingertip, starting with the outside of the little finger and finishing with the inside of the index-finger. Stretch your hands and your thumb and fingers outwards. Now go back the other way. Repeat eighteen times then switch to the other hand.

You can progress to doing this exercise at speed and flexing both hands at the same time once you've got the hang of it.

This exercise develops sensitivity as well as helping keep your hands flexible and is popular with musicians. It is also said to stimulate qi in the acupuncture channels which end at the fingertips.

The Pelvic Floor

If you are going to do great tai chi, your pelvis needs to move very freely. You therefore have to have mobile hips and a relaxed pelvic floor, which will support your organs and allow you to develop your "root". In correct posture, your pelvis is like a basin which holds up your entire upper body and it is therefore imperative that it is correctly aligned. Any misalignment can cause a variety of unexplained symptoms including lack of enjoyment of sexual intercourse, as well as preventing you from moving correctly when you do your tai chi.

Most women, especially those who have given birth, will know about "Kegel" exercises, designed to keep the muscles of the pelvic floor from collapsing as they get older. But a problem which is of great relevance to tai chi practitioners is that of a hypertonic, or too tense pelvic floor. The muscles need to be strong but supple.

You may find yourself being instructed to hold up the perineum when doing qi gong or tai chi. This process is not unlike the "Kegel" and is beneficial for the pelvic floor. The perineum is the area between your genitals and anus, the Hui Yin point in acupuncture. This is an important gate for qi flow and it can be easily blocked by tension in the body.

The goal of the following exercises is to release tension and develop the connection between the pelvis and the other parts of your body.

The pelvis is your centre of gravity, home of the dantian and the controller of all movement, as any tai chi book will tell you.

Apart from the exercise below, you may want to think about trying to relax your perineum using internal massage. Mothers may have been advised on techniques, as relaxation of this area can help prevent the skin from tearing when giving birth. Otherwise, you can find instructions on the internet for both female and male techniques. If you have a partner you may be able to interest them in helping you.

Note

If you have pelvic pain, incontinence or dysfunction you should see your doctor.

Floor Ball

Sit down either on the floor or a hard chair, (the latter is probably the less unpleasant option) with your trusty tennis ball positioned beneath the perineum. Gently allow your weight to rest on the ball and stay in position for five or ten minutes. Repeat daily.

This will almost certainly be quite uncomfortable to begin with, but it relaxes the pelvic floor muscles and the discomfort should improve fairly quickly.

At Work

Whatever work you do, the chances are these days that you'll have some kind of automated help. Computers, telephones, electronic equipment, machinery, in all walks of life there are devices designed to make humans more efficient and speed up the process by which they perform their tasks.

These devices can also cause a number of problems, including but not limited to neck, shoulder and backache, carpal tunnel syndrome and other cumulative trauma disorders (that's RSI to me and you), eye disorders and headaches.

Your employers should in theory carry out workplace assessments and tackle such matters as position and lighting, but a lot of them will be paying only lip service to their responsibilities and it's important that you also take responsibility for ensuring that you're as comfortable as possible.

Regular breaks are very important. Don't kid yourself that you don't need lunch and can sit at your desk for four hours at a stretch. Research has shown that people are more productive if they take time away from their work, especially by going outside for a walk.

During breaks, you can do a few of the exercises in the Stretching section of this book. Look at it as tai chi warm-up time. You can supplement these with some stretches at your workstation.

If you're unfortunate enough to be unable or unwilling to leave it, please do these at least. Not many organisations will stop their employees from working too hard, but there also aren't many who are known for their sympathy towards workers with chronic physical conditions.

The following exercises are designed for office workers, because that's what I used to be, but they could also be used by others, including people seated for long periods at tills, industrial workstations or in vehicles.

Seated Neck Stretch

Tuck your chin in firmly (think double chin) and bring your head forward. Cup your hands around the back of your head and try to push it forward in a straight line, whilst keeping your chin in position. Hold for a minute, making sure you are breathing easily with your diaphragm. You should feel a stretch at the base of your neck and perhaps down your spine.

Side Neck Stretch

Again make a double chin. Keeping your neck upright drop your head towards your shoulder, so that the movement comes from the base of the skull, not the neck. Use the hand on the same side to push the head gently towards the shoulder whilst with the other hand you point your middle finger and push the whole arm down towards the floor. Hold and repeat on the other side. Make sure your breathing is relaxed. This exercise stretches the scalene muscles.

Note

Don't do the neck exercises if you suffer from osteoarthritis. Make sure you are sitting comfortably and evenly. Be careful not to stretch too forcefully and make sure you keep your chin tucked in.

Seated Neck Stretch　　　　　*Side Neck Stretch*

Squeezing

"Stress relievers", are small malleable toys often found in offices. They are usually round and filled with foam rubber or gel. (You can make your own with a balloon and some sand or flour or even use your tennis ball.) They may help with RSI by relaxing the arm muscles as well as having a soothing effect caused by the squeezing motion and their ability to keep your hands busy.

Making Fists

Extend your hands out straight with fingers and thumbs extended backwards, then form a fist with your fingers bent against the palm and thumb over the index and middle fingers. Extend them again, then make a half fist with fingers and thumb bent at the first joint rather than the knuckle. Extend again. Hold each position for ten seconds and repeat the sequence five times.

This exercise may help alleviate the symptoms of carpal tunnel syndrome and it improves mobility as well as strengthening the muscles of the wrist and hand. Some people find the half fist tricky to make, and as it is used in some tai chi forms it is worth mastering.

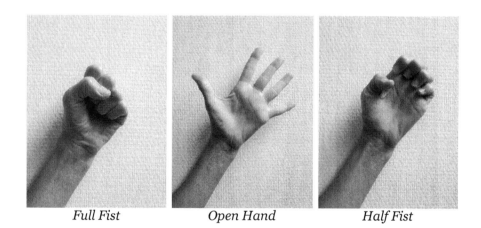

Full Fist   *Open Hand*   *Half Fist*

Eyes

Eye exercises are purported to improve your eyesight or at least prevent it from deteriorating and this is also one of the health benefits claimed for tai chi, though as far as I know there's little evidence for either claim. However, relaxing the eyes is certainly necessary when working with computer and other electronic screens and I have therefore included a couple of exercises here.

Try to remember to blink regularly and keep the screen brightness level as low as possible.

Eye Rolling

Roll your eyes in a clockwise circle, then back the other way. Blink and do it again. Now move your eyes from side to side and up and down. Blink. Repeat this exercise nine times.

Well Focused

Focus your eyes on a object as far away as possible (over 50m if you can), then shift your eyes to an object very close to you (not your computer screen!) without moving your head. Look at each for about 10 seconds and repeat nine times, moving your eyes back and forwards between the two objects.

More Stretching...

Any of the Upper Body or Shoulder Stretches from the Stretching Section of this book can be easily adapted for a seated position.

Posture

Unfortunately, the majority of activities these days in both work and leisure require greater use of the chest than the back muscles (writing, reading, lifting, gardening, driving, playing a musical instrument and working with tools to name a few examples). The shoulders tend to fall forward naturally under their own weight and the jaw to jut forward and the result is round shoulders and a head which is not held erect. This condition can also be a result of lack of confidence, which tai chi should help to address.

For correcting the physical problem, the following exercise may be of help.

The Plank

Okay, you probably won't be able to do this one in the office. I have found weight benches in gyms work well, or you may be able to improvise another solution such as that shown in the photo. (Make sure the plank can hold your weight!)

Lie down on your back with legs bent on a flat surface about 600cm (2ft) high and approximately the width of your back. Take two 1kg weights, tins of soup, 500ml bottles of water or similar items (they should both be the same). Put one weight in each hand and let your arms fall out to the sides, hands facing up. Rest in this position for five or ten minutes, checking regularly that your body is straight, your chin tucked in and your lower back as close to touching the plank as possible. Let your hands touch the floor if they can.

When you've finished bring your arms together and slowly get down (you can first place the weights on the floor if you wish).

This exercise stretches the pectoral muscles in the chest. As well as feeling taller with a more open chest, you may feel a sensation like pins and needles in your hands for a little while after doing this exercise. It should dissipate quickly.

The Plank

Reverse Plank

Reverse Plank

Lie face down on your bench with arms straight out to the sides, level and in line with the tops of your shoulders. Hold for thirty seconds and repeat five times. You can also move the arms slightly up and down, towards ceiling and floor instead of just holding.

This stretches the muscles in your back between the shoulder blades. (These two exercises should be done together – remember that you should always stretch antagonist muscles.)

Afterword

Doing tai chi is a wonderful way to get to know yourself. You may decide to keep it as a small but important part of your life, or to expand your mind and spirit as the practice leads you along unexpected and intriguing paths.

By using the exercises here, any student, whether they are a beginner or have many years' experience, can improve their tai chi. Without training to open the joints, stretch the muscles and relax the whole body, it is impossible to perform tai chi at a high level. The mind must also be calm and thoughts ordered. Having goals and concentrating on them will help you to achieve this.

It's a long process with progress often coming in tiny increments. It's useful to get someone to video you doing your form from time to time so you can see the difference in your movements. This is also a very good way of picking up faults you hadn't noticed. I remember a teacher saying that he had videoed his students and played the film to them the following week in class. He expected them to be embarrassed by their performance but in fact they had the opposite reaction, most finding that they moved and looked better than they had expected.

It's good to feel positive about your tai chi. If you are too critical of yourself you will find it hard to relax. Tai chi should be fun, not a chore. Think about doing a task you don't like: it's then that you tense your muscles, grip things tightly and screw up your face. If you're having fun the chances are you're relaxed in body and mind. Try to develop your "inner smile", the sort of expression which will only come if the muscles in your face are relaxed. (Think of the Buddha or Mona Lisa.) You should be enjoying every moment.

That said, don't be too self-satisfied. There will always be something more you can learn or improve upon. Being complacent, you don't seek to develop and will stagnate.   It's said that tai chi takes more than one lifetime to perfect – that's what makes it so interesting.

References

1. Back Pain

    http://www.nhs.uk/news/2014/03March/Pages/Back-pain-leading-cause-of-disability-study-finds.aspx

2. Chinese Literacy

    http://www.nytimes.com/2001/02/12/news/12iht-rchina.t.html

3. Yang Chengfu: *The Essence & Applications of Taijiquan,* USA: Blue Snake Books,2005

4. Studying Tai Chi in China

    http://www.china-taichi-guide.com/

5. Air Quality in China

    http://www.greenpeace.org/eastasia/news/blog/bad-to-worse-ranking-74-chinese-cities-by-air/blog/48181/

6. Water Intake Recommendations
    http://www.efsa.europa.eu/sites/default/files/scientificoutput/files/maindocuments/1459.pdf

Further Reading

Mary Bond	The New Rules of Posture: How to Sit, Stand, and Move in the Modern world
Michael Buhr	Secrets of the Pelvis for Martial Arts: A Practical Guide for Improving your Wujifa, Taiji, Xingyi, Bagua and Everyday Life
Bruce Frantzis	Taoist Sexual Meditation
Daniel Keown	The Spark in the Machine: How the Science of Acupuncture Explains the Mysteries of Western Medicine
Terry Laughlin	Total Immersion: The Revolutionary Way to Swim Better, Faster & Easier
Alexander Lowen & Leslie Lowen	The Way to Vibrant Health
Alexander Lowen	Fear of Life
Steven Shaw & Armand D'Angour	The Art of Swimming: A New Direction Using the Alexander Technique
Davidine Sim & David Gaffney	Chen Style Taijiquan: The Source of Taiji Boxing
Brad Walker	Ultimate Guide to Stretching & Flexibility
Yang Jwing Ming	Tai Chi Chuan Classical Yang Style
Yang Jwing Ming	Tai Chi Secrets of the Ancient Masters

20754513R00092

Printed in Poland
by Amazon Fulfillment
Poland Sp. z o.o., Wrocław